THE
OGLALA
SIOUX

Warriors in Transition

by

ROBERT H. RUBY

Foreword by Glenn L. Emmons
Introduction to the Bison Books edition by
Cary C. Collins

UNIVERSITY OF NEBRASKA PRESS
LINCOLN AND LONDON

First Nebraska paperback printing: 2010

Library of Congress Cataloging-in-Publication Data
Ruby, Robert H.
The Oglala Sioux: warriors in transition / Robert H. Ruby; foreword by
Glenn L. Emmons; introduction to the Bison Books edition by Cary C. Collins.
p.   cm.
Originally published: New York: Vantage Press, 1955.
Includes bibliographical references and index.
ISBN 978-0-8032-2622-7 (pbk.: alk. paper)
1. Oglala Indians—History.   2. Oglala Indians—Social life and customs.
3. Oglala Indians—Folklore.   I. Title.
E99.O3R8   2010
978.004'975244—dc22
2009049760

This Bison Books edition follows the original in beginning chapter 1 on arabic
page 13; no material has been omitted.

INTRODUCTION TO THE BISON BOOKS EDITION

Cary C. Collins

Sometime in the middle part of August 1953, Robert H. Ruby MD, a St. Louis University–trained surgeon, navigated his car for the first time into the windswept, sunburned plains of the Pine Ridge Indian Reservation in southwestern South Dakota. A few days later, in a staff meeting made up entirely of Indian agency officials and department heads, Dr. Ruby was unexpectedly named medical officer in charge of Pine Ridge Hospital, a forty-six bed medical-surgical unit operated under the authority of the Bureau of Indian Affairs (BIA). Ruby occupied that important administrative post for the next eighteen months, a period during which he served as a key figure in delivering health care to the predominantly Oglala Sioux who lived at Pine Ridge. He also functioned in a less formal capacity: as an uncommonly dedicated observer of both Indian culture and the shocking level of socioeconomic ills—a number of which have persisted to the current day—that were pervasive throughout the Pine Ridge community in the 1950s.[1]

In some ways, Ruby presented the image of a different kind of government official. In contrast to so many of his predecessors and contemporaries, he exhibited a keen interest in the Oglalas and in their history and culture. Acting on those impulses, he befriended members of the Oglala Sioux Tribe and, over the course of his tenure, managed to win a measure of their confidence and trust. He pulled them into his social sphere (at the time a very rare overture of goodwill among federal employees), and in turn they extended to him an unusual level of access to their world, allowing Ruby—among other concessions—to record in writing and capture on film their most sacred spiritual and religious ceremonies and rituals. Ruby kept a comprehensive, almost exhaustive daily diary of everything that he saw. In 1955, shortly after he left the Pine Ridge Reservation, he published *The Oglala Sioux: Warriors in Transition*, a slim volume that documented some of the history of the Oglala Sioux as well as aspects of their culture, the major problems that were plaguing them in the middle half of the twentieth century, and Ruby's recommendations for addressing and alleviating those concerns.

There was nothing that could have prepared Ruby for his experience and the daunting challenges that were to confront him at Pine Ridge. He grew up in the 1920s and 1930s on a modest farm in eastern Washington State set in the shadow of the Cascade Mountains. He attended local schools there and proved a good student and talented writer, gaining his introduction into that arena by working as a reporter for his high school newspaper. After graduation in 1939, Ruby attended Whitworth College (now University) in Spokane, where he majored in premed. From there, he entered the Washington University School of Medicine (in St. Louis, Missouri), graduating in 1945 and then completing a nine-month internship in Detroit before being inducted into the U.S. Army Air Corps. For twenty months, he served with American Occupation forces in Japan. Then, after taking his discharge, Ruby began his studies to become a surgeon. He accepted a fellowship at the Sugarbaker Cancer Clinic in Jefferson City, Missouri, and completed a year of postgraduate training at Washington University. Putting the finishing touches on his education, he spent four years of residency in pathology and general surgery at a hospital in St. Louis.[2]

At the outbreak of the Korean War, Ruby was called back into the military. To his relief, however, a provision contained in the federal draft law granted physicians in residency their preference of service that could be delayed until the completion of that specialized training, and Ruby benefited from that opportunity. Upon finishing his residency, Ruby was assigned to the Pine Ridge Reservation, where, as a physician in the Public Health Service and newly married, he and his wife established their first home. Ruby described that turn of events in dramatic phrases: "It is almost like a nightmare to even think of what my last fifty years would have been like had one of the many decisions necessary to get [me] to . . . Pine Ridge . . . been different. What a terrific life I would have missed."[3]

Ruby arrived in 1953, stayed a year and a half, and left deeply affected. Most immediately, Pine Ridge projected vivid images of grinding poverty. Many inhabitants of the reservation, members of the Oglala Sioux Tribe, lived in shacks and some only in tents—a sorry state of affairs that afforded the people virtually no protection from the extreme weather that ranged from blistering summer heat to arctic winter cold. In addition, crime and alcoholism were rampant. Although federal law prohibited the selling of intoxicants on the reservation, several taverns located south just across the Nebraska state line in Whiteclay operated without any restriction. Finally, the reservation appeared jarringly out of step with modern industrial society. Few Oglalas owned cars, and at a time when the federal interstate highway system was beginning to fan out across the nation, horses and horse-drawn wagons remained visible sights at Pine Ridge.

Within this environment, Ruby forged tight bonds with many of the Indians with whom he came into contact. At first finding the Oglalas reticent and withdrawn in their encounters with him and with non-Indians generally, Ruby made it a point to interact with them and set them at ease. Notably, he and his wife—who taught at Oglala Community High School in Pine Ridge—became the first agency employees to entertain Indians in their home, an extension of hospitality and kindness that, in addition to her teaching and his health care, helped win over the Oglalas. It also drew the Rubys into close associations with many of the most prominent members of the tribe, particularly those of the Red Cloud, Black Elk, and Standing Bear families—the children and grandchildren of those famous Lakota leaders.

The rich historical backdrop of Pine Ridge was a catalyst that

helped to launch Ruby as a lifetime writer of books. The Indian
agency was located just twelve miles from the Wounded Knee massacre site, and Ruby began questioning the Oglalas about their
history and culture. He also started attending cultural events. Of
special appeal to him were those holding religious relevance. Most
interestingly, Ruby became the first white person on the Pine Ridge
Reservation to witness a ceremony of the Native American Church
(Peyotism), and he was the only non-Indian allowed to take pictures inside their house of worship. Such was the unbridled, un-
disguised nature of Ruby's enthusiasm for the Oglalas that he says
the two groups of Peyotism on the reservation—Half Moon and
Cross Fire—began competing against one another to have him as a
guest at their services, even to the point of threatening to seize him
hostage in order to insure his presence. Today Dr. Ruby doesn't
feel that achieving the acceptance of the Oglalas was something
"he really had to work hard at," but rather his relationships with
them "gradually evolved over time." After a while, he explains, the
Oglalas "could see that I was someone who could be trusted . . .
that I was someone genuinely interested in meeting with them and
learning about them and their culture."[4]

Along with his numerous duties as medical officer in charge,
and in addition to the considerable time and energy that he was de-
voting to maintaining a meticulous diary of his everyday activities
and the sights and sounds of the reservation, Dr. Ruby began pre-
paring a manuscript that was intended for publication. The project
emerged as a logical extension of what he already had been doing.
According to Ruby, he was always in constant contact and conver-
sation with the Oglalas, and when he and his wife had them in
their residence for dancing, storytelling, music, and feasting, Ruby
took copious notes of what was said. "I just kept talking to them,
particularly [to the Oglala artist] Jake Herman," Ruby remembers.
"They told me the Indian spellings for the words used in the book,
and I was also able to include all of my direct observations of the
meetings I was attending out on the reservation."[5] Ruby kept a camera at the ready at the hospital, and when a patient would drop in
whom he considered to be of historical stature, he would ask to
snap their picture. He also consigned several Lakota artists to paint

for him—including Herman, Andrew Standing Soldier, and Felix Walking—and it goes almost without saying that the illustrative material contained in this reprint offers just a sliver of the several hundred kodachrome slides and numerous other historical and artistic objects that Ruby either produced or acquired at Pine Ridge.[6]

When he was ready to go public with his writing, Ruby looked to only one publisher, Vantage Press, which he contacted from Pine Ridge in the latter half of 1954. Later, on a visit to New York City for a meeting of the American College of Surgeons, Ruby took a few moments to sit down with the editors in their offices there in order to solidify their relationship. The book was finally released in the summer of 1955, after Ruby had vacated Pine Ridge and relocated to Moses Lake, Washington, where, by then, he was engaged in private surgical practice. *The Oglala Sioux* contained only 115 pages and received limited circulation (it was actually a self-publication for which Ruby invested over $1,000 of his own money; the book sold for $2.50 a copy), but it signaled the passage of a milestone: Ruby was now an author in print. The volume also proved timely, providing the Smithsonian Institution with the pictures and text for a Plains Indian exhibit that was under construction in Washington DC.

The Oglala Sioux offered a unique approach and also filled a void in the literature available on Lakota history and culture. Dr. Ruby's documenting of the Pine Ridge Reservation and the Oglala Sioux Tribe was the product of a highly educated and extremely interested observer, but one who lacked many of the professional qualifications typically possessed by those undertaking such work. For example, prior to his time at Pine Ridge Ruby had never lived on an Indian reservation, could boast no experience working with Indians, knew little or nothing of federal Indian policies, and possessed no formal training in the various disciplines of history, ethnology, or anthropology. By necessity, therefore, his was very much a case of learning on the run, with Ruby having to devise his own strategies for classifying, preserving, and making sense of the substantial amounts of data he was gathering.

In a similar vein, Dr. Ruby came to Pine Ridge lacking any working knowledge of Oglala culture or spiritual beliefs and practices

and, like anyone in his situation, was able to process and assimi-
late only a fraction of everything he took in. Thus, even with him
throwing himself into the daunting task of amassing as much understanding as was humanly feasible, his findings and conclusions
could not be construed as those of a trained academic, one who
might have spent years, or decades, living on the reservation studying the Oglala people, their culture, and their lifeways. Ruby was
also prone to inserting his own viewpoints and commentaries into
his writing, freely sharing his opinions on what he believed needed
to be done to lessen the suffering of the Oglalas. It was an assertive-
ness that derived from both the innate straightforwardness of his
personality and the demands that had been thrust upon him in his
supervisory role as the head of Pine Ridge Hospital.

For Ruby, however, in weakness there was strength. Those defin-
ing, raw, first-person, in-the-heat-of-the-moment qualities imbued
his work with a distinctiveness seldom seen in other publications
of the period. Ruby operated on his own experiences, of which he
was both an onlooker and participant. By the authority vested in
him through his office as hospital administrator, Ruby had an obligation to uphold federal policies that were continuing to heavily
regulate Indian tribes. At the same time, he was helping—and often struggling—to formulate and implement programs that could
bring a higher standard of services and health care to the Oglala
people. Hence, he was no simple bystander; he was an active per-
former moving among the Oglala people, an important mediator
in the daily drama that he was so assiduously documenting. What
Ruby lacked in professional cache he made up for in standing and
in his strategic positioning as a key functionary in the federal bu-
reaucracy at Pine Ridge.

Ruby labored at Pine Ridge at the height of a monumental
shift that was underway in federal Indian policy. The longtime na-
tional impetus of institutionalized assimilation had finally given
way to what would come to be known as the Indian New Deal. The
latter restored much of the cultural sovereignty that had been lost
under the former policy, but it also failed to free Indians from the
tight yoke of the BIA. This was especially the case in terms of the
tribal governments, constitutions, and bylaws established under

BIA authority in the 1930s. However, after the Second World War and in the 1950s, new initiatives, known as termination (originally called withdrawal) and relocation, began to usurp those principles embodied in the Indian New Deal. Termination policy sought to sever the fundamental and, in no small number of cases, treaty-sanctioned federal-tribal trust relationships that had been established, along with many of the solemn obligations of health and welfare that had stood as the hallmarks of the government's long oversight of Indian affairs. Relocation aimed to move Indians off reservations and into cities, where they would receive training before being integrated into the economic and social mainstream.

The emergence of termination and relocation meshed with the views that would come to be those of Robert Ruby. His obligations as medical officer in charge exacted a debilitating physical and psychological toll on him, and by 1955 Ruby was, by his own admission, a frustrated, disillusioned government administrator. Over the course of his term at Pine Ridge, Ruby increasingly struggled to reconcile what he thought *should* be happening with what was *actually* taking place on the ground. For him (and for his immediate supervisor, the superintendent of Pine Ridge Agency, Ben Reifel), Indians had become overly dependent on government programs and services, a development that—in the minds of Ruby and Reifel—was working to the detriment of the Oglalas. In his diary, Ruby voiced with mounting fervor and frequency his displeasure at the conditions he was constantly running up against. Some of the blame for that he laid squarely at the feet of federal Indian policies, but some was also reserved for the Oglalas, whom Ruby took to task for doing too little, he thought at the time, to provide for their own health and welfare. Strains of that venting found their way into *The Oglala Sioux*.[7]

A subject of particular interest to Ruby, and one that consumed much of his research and space in *The Oglala Sioux*, was Lakota spirituality. Ruby enjoyed intimate contact with the leaders of all Native religions on the Pine Ridge Reservation, and he attended their meetings and services, including those of Yuwipe, the Native American Church (both Cross Fire and Half Moon), and Sun Dance ceremonies. Each of those had been severely restricted during the soul-wrenching heyday of American Indian policies of assimilation (dating from approximately 1880 to 1933) but had re-emerged active and seemingly vibrant in the middle 1950s. Ruby, as he did wherever he went on the reservation, gained permission to take pictures. Then, either during the live event or shortly after he returned to his office at the hospital or his house in the village of Pine Ridge, he produced meticulous notes of what he had seen. Ruby prepared his text on a typewriter, which he augmented with hand-drawn sketches that illustrated details such as the layout of the meeting room, the positioning of the altar and the chairs or benches, and any other paraphernalia or ornamentation that seemed important.

Indian spirituality was a point of veneration but also concern. Ruby, as in almost everything that he experienced at Pine Ridge, found himself torn between the admiration he felt for the residents of the Pine Ridge Reservation (almost all of whom were his patients), his obligations toward them as a federal agent, and what he personally believed to be in the best long-term interests of the tribe. For example, in *The Oglala Sioux* Ruby evinced genuine respect as he shared some of what he had observed at various religious events on the reservation, but he related, too, his unwavering conviction that Lakota spirituality stood as an obstacle to tribal members taking full advantage of the services offered at Pine Ridge Hospital. Similarly, it was with great pride that he spoke about Lakota history and the marshal prowess of the Oglalas, but at the same time he viewed their past as a hindrance to their quick and forceful assimilation into the dominant society of the 1950s. Like many non-Indians at midcentury, Ruby perceived a fundamental incompatibility between Indian culture and the demands of an increasingly industrial, market-driven economy.

The decision of the University of Nebraska Press to make available this reprint of *The Oglala Sioux* speaks to the book's shifting importance in the canon of texts written on the tribe. With the passage of fifty-five years since the date of its original publication, *The Oglala Sioux* is no longer a survey of current conditions as it was back in 1955. Rather, it is a historical document that can be read with the hindsight of everything that has transpired on the reservation in the last five and a half decades. When Dr. Ruby was at Pine Ridge, the nation was teetering on the verge of undergoing a revolution in its treatment of minorities, while the destitution and despair, the problems and tensions referenced by Ruby, were on the brink of erupting full force and engulfing the Pine Ridge Reservation in the Civil Rights and Red Power movements of the late 1960s and early 1970s. The seeds of those encounters can be detected in *The Oglala Sioux*; the tribe was attempting—not always successfully—to cope with a century of failed government policies and programs, as well as a health care system that had proved abysmally inadequate and that, like the entire BIA system, sat on the cusp of complete reorganization and restructuring.

Today *The Oglala Sioux* opens a window onto the Pine Ridge Reservation during a pivotal period of recovery, transition, and survival—a period when the Oglala Sioux Tribe was trying to sustain as much of its history and culture as it could while also striving to incorporate into the lives of its members elements of the larger American society as waves of rapid change were sweeping through both the reservation and the country. Dr. Ruby was there at the height of those challenging times, leaving his own imprint as a health care professional while documenting for future generations what it was he was seeing and hearing, articulating the views of a BIA administrator during the hollow days of termination and relocation. Through his tireless efforts of data collection, a lasting record—preserved in multiple mediums—has been left that otherwise would have been lost, and for that we are all beneficiaries.

NOTES

1. Robert H. Ruby's experiences at Pine Ridge are documented in Robert H. Ruby, *A Doctor among the Oglala Sioux Tribe: The Letters of Robert H. Ruby, 1953–1954*, ed. Cary C. Collins and Charles V. Mutschler (Lincoln: University of Nebraska Press, 2010). Biographical background on Ruby is found in Cary C. Collins and Charles V. Mutschler, "'Thank God They Did What They Did When They Did': Ruby and Brown and the Writing of American Indian History," *Journal of the West* 46, no. 2 (Spring 2007): 3–10; and Collins and Mutschler, "Great Spirits: Ruby and Brown, Pioneering Historians of the Indians of the Pacific Northwest," *Pacific Northwest Quarterly* 95, no. 3 (Summer 2004): 126–29.

2. For Ruby's college and medical background, consult Karen Sandrick, "Surgeon Chronicles Native American History," *Bulletin of the American College of Surgeons* 90, no. 11 (November 2005): 9–14.

3. Typed letter from Robert H. Ruby to Collins and Mutschler, November 20, 2003, Eastern Washington University Archives, Cheney, Washington [hereafter cited as EWUA].

4. Oral interview, Collins with Ruby, November 6, 2008, EWUA.

5. Oral interview, Collins with Ruby, August 12, 2008, EWUA.

6. Ruby has donated his art collection to Whitworth University in Spokane, Washington, and Eastern Washington University in Cheney. His personal papers and photographs are housed at the Northwest Museum of Art and Cultures, Spokane, Washington.

7. Benjamin Reifel (1906–90), a Lakota Sioux from the Rosebud Indian Reservation, served as superintendent of Pine Ridge Agency from 1953 to 1955 and as a Republican congressman from South Dakota from 1961 to 1971. Reifel was also the commissioner of Indian affairs in 1976 at the conclusion of the Gerald Ford administration.

To EDNA PHYLLIS
*who was born in the Indian hospital
on Pine Ridge*

FOREWORD

There are today more than 250 Indian tribal groups in the United States. Of this large number, the Dakota, or Sioux, Indians stand high in the imaginations of the non-Indian people of the country. The fierce courage of the Sioux in battle, and the determination with which they long clung to their lands and resisted the encroachment of the white man and his civilization, colors the pages of our history books.

In the early days the Sioux were largely a misunderstood and greatly feared tribe. The very mention of their name was enough to send shudders down the spines of the timid and the brave alike. Yet, like many other tribes in the days of the settlement of the United States, they fought for what was theirs and were attacked as often—perhaps more often—than they attacked.

Today they remain an easily misunderstood group. They have continued to resist much of the white man's civilization, accepting that which is useful to them and rejecting whatever they feel is not good for the Sioux, or anything which might in some way change them from Sioux to white men. They are, in other words, clearly and proudly Indian; and there will always be, I believe, men among them who will strive to lift them above the stigma of degeneracy and keep aflame in their hearts all that the name Sioux stands for—courage, determination, and strength.

In THE OGLALA SIOUX: *Warriors in Transition*, Dr. Ruby has told their story with a warmth of understanding too seldom accorded a group of Americans who need and deserve all the patience and help necessary to make the difficult transition that their country offers them.

February 2, 1955

GLENN L. EMMONS
Commissioner of Indian Affairs

CONTENTS

INTRODUCTION

BEFORE WORKING FOR the Bureau of Indian Affairs, I had no idea that there was an isolated group of people in our midst—the Indians—who were beset with so many peculiar problems.

In South Dakota, on the Pine Ridge Indian Reservation, the second largest in the country, live the Oglala Sioux, still observing customs and clinging to habits that served the needs of their ancestors over one hundred years ago. They are held so tenaciously by their old superstitions that they all but refuse to accept the basic standards of modern civilization.

The Sioux Nation was once a powerful body. Today, as in the past, it comprises three main groups. Within each group are several tribes, and within the tribes are various bands. The three great divisions by language are the Santee, the Yankton, and the Teton Sioux: the Santees are the Nekotas; the Yanktons, the Dakotas; and the Tetons, the Lakotas.

The Oglalas are one of seven tribes of the Teton Sioux. The other six are the Brule, Minneconjou, Hunkpapa (not the Hunkpatilas, who were a band of Oglalas), No Bows, Two Kettles, and Blackfoot. Within the Oglala tribe are many bands, each of which was once led by a chief.

This short book has been prepared from letters recounting personal experiences of the Indians, from which have been culled bits of folklore and history, and stories I learned from the Indians themselves. I have used reference books only to confirm dates, to arrange in chronological order the events in the lives of Chiefs Crazy Horse and Red Cloud, and to check stories of the Battle of Wounded Knee, which is still a highly controversial affair. Otherwise, the stories are the Indians'.

The opinions expressed are my own. If they are held by others, it is only that I share them. In no way are they intended to represent those of the Bureau of Indian Affairs. There may be many people who will not agree with the opinions I have given in the last chapter of this book. I can only assume that they probably have not had the experience of living and dealing with the Indians, day after day, for a long period.

Sentimentality will not help the Indian. I listen with displeasure to the sentimentalists who romanticize Indian violations of the past. This emotional attitude does not help the Indian today. This is 1955. The Indians are American citizens who must be fitted into our contemporary society.

The problems on Pine Ridge are real. They must be dealt with in terms of the present. Only a realistic approach to the Indians' problems can help them to the level of civilization on which they can cope with the "outside" world.

But this digresses from the purpose of the larger part of this book. In considering the problems of a people and the motives for their actions, no study could be valid without some knowledge of their historical and cultural background. To fill in some of the less known details of this background is my aim.

All references to Indians in the following pages are to the Oglala Sioux unless otherwise qualified. This is important to bear in mind, as there are many tribes of Indians in the United States that are integrated into non-Indian society, and much of what is here set forth does not hold true elsewhere.

                                                              R. H. R.

The Oglala Sioux

Chapter I

THE OLD AND THE NEW

(SAMPI YAYA LE HANTU)

THE OGLALA SIOUX INDIANS of today are not like their ancestors of one hundred years ago, but they have remained a picturesque people. Many primitive customs and religious rituals survive, and the old crafts are still practiced. But the mixing of old traditions with an imposed new culture has not been happy. It has resulted in a confused people.

The Sioux stand apart from other American Indian tribes in several ways. They have produced colorful, fascinating, and stormy leaders. They were made famous by "Buffalo Bill" Cody, who took them on tours through the United States and Europe. Their resistance to the white man and the federal government, longer than any other tribe, gave them great notoriety. In the last open clashes between whites and Indians, the Sioux were the Indians. And today, although this also applies to a few other tribes in some respects, the Sioux still cling to their old superstitions and cultures with stubborn persistence. Their lives, attitudes, and practices are a mixture of primitive habits, sifted through modern teachings and customs, which has produced a complex tribal personality. Of the Indians living on the reservation, the proportion

13

of full bloods to half-breeds and mixed bloods is approximately fifteen per cent to eighty-five per cent. Family names are essentially Indian, with a fair proportion of French names and a sprinkling of Irish, Mexican, and Scandinavian names, a heritage of the squaw men.

Before the white man disturbed the Plains Indians, the Sioux, in small bands, roamed through Minnesota, the Dakotas, Wyoming, Colorado, and Utah. They provided for their essential needs partly by means of their own, limited stone-age implements, but their thievery from other Indian tribes was notorious. The word *Sioux* means cutthroat. The name came from the Chippewa tribe. The early white men who went into the area asked the Chippewas who the Plains Indians were. Since the Chippewas had been at war with the Lakotas they told the white men their enemies were Sioux, or cutthroats. (The tribe name is Lakota, and they refer to themselves by this name.)

Before the scalping era, the Lakotas used to slit the throats of their captive enemies. The word *Sioux* is derived from the French. The sign language for the Sioux tribe is made by drawing the hand across the neck, to indicate cutting a throat.

The Sioux were always at war with the Crows of Montana and the Snakes, and after the Chippewas were forced west, into Minnesota and North Dakota, they warred against them too. The Sioux warrior was adept at sneaking, during the night, into the camp of a different tribe, and running off with the best horses. And if he learned to do the work by daylight, he became a celebrated brave. Thieving within one's own band was a crime, prohibited by tribal moral code. Thieving from other tribes was considered honorable and praiseworthy.

More hostile to the whites than other Plains Indians, the Sioux put up the fiercest resistance to the westward march of civilization. *Wasicu* is the Lakota for white man. The original meaning was "can't get rid of them." When a warrior or camp scout returned to the band from an observation post, he was asked for an account of what he had seen. He would first roll his fingers into the palm of his hand, with his thumb pointed up. This meant that he was giving the truth. (A false statement was indicated with the thumb turned down.) The scout might then tell that on the first ridge were a few buffalo, on the next ridge were many, and on the farthest ridge there were so many buffalo that one could shoot many arrows and *Wasicu,* (never get rid of them.) This apparently was the original meaning of the word now used to define white people.

In the days before the white man's coming only a minimum amount of an Indian family's time went toward procuring food, clothing, and other household needs. The rest of the time was spent warring, celebrating, feasting, and dancing. The Indian had no medium of exchange. A man's wealth was determined by the number of horses he owned.

There was no incentive to work to accumulate material possessions. The Indian had no philosophy about improving his lot, or keeping up with his neighbors. Consequently the Sioux today prefers to adhere to this old way of living. He would rather not work, yet he has a fondness for two of the white man's possessions, liquor and the automobile. Electric lights, stoves, and refrigerators are nice, but families living on the reservation are content to live in a small log hut or frame shack so small that it would fit comfortably into the living room of a modern house. They burn wood and kerosene. The average home is lighted by kerosene lamps. The only furniture is a stove, a table, bed, and few chairs.

The Sioux never stayed very long in one place; they roamed continually. Tepees made of animal hides served for shelter. At one time, the Sioux used the chow dog harnessed to a travois for hauling family possessions. Their trips were called "walking days," before they acquired horses.

Since 1951, the Bureau of Indian Affairs has been carrying out a program that aims at placing any family that wants to become integrated into average American life in a large city, away from the reservation, where jobs are found for its members. So far, more than sixty per cent of these "rehabilitated and relocated" Indian families have become homesick for the communal way of life and have returned to the reservations.

Many Indians today belong to one or another of the denominational Christian churches. But there are few who take their religion seriously enough to abandon their old beliefs. Some adhere to Yuwipi, the old Sioux Indian religion. Others belong to the Native American Church, which incorporates the old religion and Christianity, and is also the peyote cult. The Indians are superstitious. They mix their beliefs. Some practice either Yuwipi or Native American Church, and attend a Christian church also. Many Indians like going to church; it gives them a chance to meet and congregate. They enjoy eating. And many depend on the church for clothing.

In their hearts, the Sioux are not entirely friendly to the white man. They take out much of their resentment on federal employees. Mothers drill into their youngsters' minds the sufferings and wrongs inflicted upon the Indians in times past, in the Battle of Wounded Knee and the massacre of the Indians by Colonel Forsythe's men, in the winter of 1890, for instance. They tell them how the white men took the gold from the Black Hills, killed the buffalo, appropriated the land and shoved the people onto reservations, killed them wantonly, and broke peace treaties whenever it suited their purposes.

Early Sioux leaders with whom the Long Knives (the federal soldiers) had to deal were Red Cloud, Crazy Horse, Red Shirt, Rain-in-the-Face, Spotted Tail, Crow King, American Horse, Gall, Sitting Bull, Little Wound, Bad Wound. All were chiefs except Sitting Bull. He was a shaman though he also was a shrewd and powerful leader, who had the devotion and following of his people.

In 1866, after much harassment from the Teton Sioux, the federal government sued for peace so that the Bozeman Trail could be built. The trail would link the gold fields near Virginia City, Montana, to the Union Pacific railroad. But when the white men began to build forts, Chief Red Cloud and his band started a war against the whites.

The treaty of 1868 granted the Sioux Nation (all tribes) a large expanse of land that would not be trespassed; this included the Black Hills and the land east of the Missouri River. The white men promised that forts and roads would not be built across the Indian land. They received the right to build roads and forts at various places off this area, across to the West, however.

In 1875, gold was discovered in the Black Hills, and the white men stampeded across the Dakotas, invading the Indians' land. The angered Indians resisted, as they retreated to Montana. The government tried to break up these hostile forces and sent in the cavalry. The clashes led to the Battle of the Little Big Horn and the death of General Custer and his men, in 1876, the Moon of Making Fat (June).

From 1877 to 1879, the Indians were sent to the Missouri River bottoms to live, while negotiations for the sale of the Hills went on between Chief Red Cloud and the palefaces. To this day, Red Cloud is held in low esteem by many Indians. They say he was drunk when he let the white man have the Hills. And when one Sioux talks to another about some current federal project that is a great expense to the government, the standard reply is "The Black Hills are paying for it."

The winter of 1878 was a lean one for the tribes lodged on the banks of the Missouri River. In the early fall, usually in the month of Calf Growing Black, a small cluster of bright stars is visible on clear nights. The Indians kept watch for this sign, for when it appeared they knew it was time to prepare for the winter. The buffalo were then fat; the berries were ripe for picking and preserving, and the horses would soon have to be turned out. But the first winter on the Missouri bottom lands was not a good season. Berries were scarce. Besides, uprooted by the recent state of affairs, the Indians had not prepared well. At times, to get food, they probed

the banks of the river with sticks, to find soft spots, which
indicated the holes of ground animals, where buried artichokes could be found.

A story is still told about this winter of hard times. It is
said that an old woman, poking in the river bank, came upon
a soft spot. Digging into it, she came upon the animal's hole,
and there found some artichokes. Just then, a small fur
animal came rushing up and said, "Old woman with knobby
fingers, why do you steal my store of artichokes?"

The old woman answered, "I didn't watch for the stars,
to prepare for my own winter's use."

In 1879, after nearly two years on the banks of the Missouri River, Red Cloud's band repaired to the present Pine
Ridge Reservation. Red Cloud didn't like the trade in fire-
water between his band and the men who were coming up
the Missouri to Pierre, on steamships. It was Red Cloud who
chose the new location, where the Pine Ridge Agency stands
today.

After the treaty of 1868, the government officially recognized several chiefs who had co-operated with federal
authorities. One of the great heroes of the Sioux is Chief
Crazy Horse, who was not among those recognized by the
federal government. Crazy Horse would make no concessions
to the white man. There is no photograph of him in existence, because he would not let the white man turn his in-
vention, the camera, on him. Crazy Horse was one of the
leaders in the Custer battle, and the government made many
attempts to imprison him. Not until September 5, 1877,
however, was he captured and killed, at Fort Robinson,
Crawford, Nebraska. When Buffalo Bill toured with the
Sioux he exhibited an Indian called Crazy Horse, but he
was not the original chief. Buffalo Bill's Crazy Horse was
the Indian who married the chief's widow, and assumed the
name.

In the early days, white men were not allowed to cross
the reservation. Even after the Indians had been subdued
on the reservation, a white man and his party could cross it

only if they had a permit. Today there are good paved state highways through the reservation.

In 1903, a white man and his family obtained a permit to cross the reservation with their horses and wagons. Among the horses was a black stallion that was unusually frisky, hard to control, and gave the man a great deal of trouble. During the journey, the party bedded down one night where Kyle is today. He visited with the Indians there, and before leaving he gave the black stallion to Antoine Herman, a mixed breed. Antoine let his eldest son tend the horse. But the old black stallion was mean. One day, as his son leaned over to pull some hay from beneath the horse's front feet, the stallion struck the boy with his hoofs, knocked him down, and then trampled him to death. The people of the community were so angered by the horse's actions that, for the first time in the history of the Sioux Nation, a council met to judge an animal. The stallion was staked. The men sat in a circle around him. After much discussion, it was agreed that he should be judged under the second offense of the unwritten criminal code, which permits a father who has lost an eldest son in battle to take his vengeance on the enemy in any way he sees fit. It was first decided to ax the stallion to death, but someone remembered Jake Walks Under the Ground, who had a reputation as an animal abuser. It was therefore decided to let Jake ride the horse to near-death, then kill him off with an ax. This was done.

The four cardinal sins of the Sioux's unwritten code were to permit anyone to be without food (this has been carried over into present-day social customs; a native Indian Bureau employee is often so swamped with relatives during the winter months that his pay check is entirely spent on groceries); to lose an eldest son in war; to permit the baby of a dead mother to cry (the cry of hunger); and for a man to return from battle alone, his comrades having been killed.

Until 1953, the Indian was not allowed by law to own firearms nor to buy and drink liquor. But most Indian families have owned guns for years. It was a law that lay dormant.

And there are many bootleggers on the reservation. The ground is littered with beer cans and beer bottles. The Indian has always obtained his liquor. Drunkenness is frequent. It is the most common offense, and keeps the tribal jail filled to capacity.

In the old days, illegitimacy and prostitution were rarely heard of. The sexual code was strict. Any maiden caught visiting behind neighboring tepees was ostracized from the group. Besides, if maidens did not remain virgins, it would be bad hunting when the buffalo season came.

Civilization has brought these people new problems. Once, a young warrior did not look his in-laws in the face, even though he lived in the same tepee with them. Social customs were such that a young man had little direct contact with any women but his wife, Law and order were not problems, years ago. The Indian did not covet material possessions to any great degree. The only reason for murder was the very infrequent instance in which a warrior stole another's wife. And if the vicitimized husband shot the thief, he was sent away from the tribe.

The first Indian from the Pine Ridge Reservation to be hanged, after trial by a white jury, was Two Sticks. It came about this way. The federal government used to give rations to all Indians, including staples, clothing, blankets, and meat. Herds of cattle were brought up from Texas and divided among the people. The cattle were kept outside the Agency at Herd Camp, today the farm headquarters for the agricultural program of the high school. This practice of distributing cattle was discontinued in 1905. In the 1890s, however, the cowboys who herded the steers distributed them to families on orders from the Agent. One night a young roughneck named Two Sticks went out to the corral that enclosed the new herd and asked the cowboy on duty for a steer. The cowboy explained that no cattle could be issued without orders from the Agent. Two Sticks became belligerent, but the cowboy continued to refuse his request. Two Sticks left, but he soon returned with four other young men.

They attacked the cowboy and four others at the camp, killing all five. The Indian police rounded up three of the attackers and shot them on the spot. Sometime later the fourth was tracked down and shot. Two Sticks was captured, tried, condemned to death, and taken to Denver, where he was hanged.

The standards of personal conduct among the Sioux show a sharp decline from the old days. Fighting and quarreling are a daily occurrence, especially in families. Divorce is frequent. Abandoned children are numerous. Juvenile delinquency is high. Illicit cohabitation and prostitution are widespread. Illegitimate births are exceptionally common, reaching a peak nine months after the late summer and early fall rodeos and roundups. Drunkenness is an everyday problem, which lies at the root of much of the trouble and misery.

The most thorough study of the Lakota language is contained in a comprehensive language manual compiled by Father Buechel, who came from Germany to the Pine Ridge Reservation in 1907. After twelve years, he was transferred one hundred miles east to the Rosebud Reservation. Father Buechel, now over eighty, lives at the St. Francis Mission, and spends much of his time studying his collection of Indian lore housed in a museum there.

Sioux history has been virtually lost except for a few occasional events. These have been only briefly recorded. Much more is known of their customs and habits, for these have been handed down by word of mouth and set down years later in manuscripts.

The Sioux did not use picture language to record events, to any great degree. They have various symbols for words, but they did not set them down on skins, except in keeping their calendar. This records only one event for each year, and the year is given a name instead of a number. The year 1861, for instance, was the year of Plenty Buffaloes. Although the white man had been wantonly destroying the animals, that year was memorable because there were still so many to be shot and preserved. The year 1865 was the year When Three Men Were Hanging at the Soldier Fort (Fort Laramie). Some Indians who retain much of the old folklore continue the tradition of naming each year, although it is done out of respect for tradition only. In 1945, when the first Indian WAC returned to the reservation, after World War II, the year was named Return of the Soldier Woman, in her honor. Years were called winters by the Indians: months were moons, and days were sleeps.

The Sioux used smoke signals for daytime messages and fire signals for nighttime communication. They used mirrors to flash messages in the bright sunlight, after the white man introduced the looking glass.

The Lakota language has no curse words. The language is not understood by other tribes, just as the Lakotas cannot understand other tribal languages. Sign language was the universal language. When tribes met for peacemaking or bargaining, this was the form of communication, performed with the hands and fingers. Sign language was used to talk with the deaf. It was also used to talk to someone at a distance. Today a perverted form of sign language is common. Nasty implications have been introduced into it. Youngsters use it in school. A white child may say, "Teacher, he said a naughty word about me," and the Indian children occasionally complain to the teacher, "He wiggled his finger at me."

The Indians also use sign language when they wish to discuss a white person in his presence. More frequently, however, they use the Lakota language.

All Indian affairs are conducted in English. Records of tribal councils are kept in English. There are no Indians who do not understand English, although some of the old full bloods speak English very poorly. There are a number who can speak English but prefer to have an interpreter when they conduct their affairs at the Agency offices. They feel they would lose face if they were to break down and conduct their own affairs in the English language.

Practically every Indian of reading age reads English.

They read newspapers, pamphlets, public notices, and bulletins. They are eager for news, and for the announcements that are sent out from the Agency. They pass along the news by word of mouth to their neighbors and friends.

The Pine Ridge Reservation is one hundred square miles of rolling hills, ravines, and isolated areas, but a news item will spread from one corner to the other three in a day's time. The Indians call their method of communication the moccasin grapevine. It is more effective than any a bureau employee might use in trying to locate someone. It is necessary only to make a public announcement that someone is wanted at the Agency office, and in short order he is present.

Homes are far apart. The yards around houses have a cleaned appearance; litter and garbage is rarely seen. Besides a privy and a squaw cooler, the yard may be filled with old cars, up to five is not unusual. The people buy old used autos, because they cannot afford new ones, and frequently pay much more than the used cars are worth. The young men run the cars for all that is in them. The cars become great oil burners before the young men discard them and look for a new bargain. The used-car dealers exploit the people. They watch for news items of families who have had land sales. An Indian with money is easy prey.

The customary way of "keeping up with the Joneses" is to own an automobile. A car is every family's greatest desire. To improve their homes or obtain good clothing are nonexistent Lakota customs.

Travel is not easy for families who do not own autos. They pay excessive charges to get a family that owns a car to bring them to the Agency to transact their business. The average fare for an eighty-mile trip is fifteen dollars. Another racket is carried on by a few who know what commodities a person is entitled to. They tell their less-knowing friends that they have influence and can obtain certain provisions for them if they are given a cut.

A horse and wagon is still a common sight. The "old

man" drives. The rest of the family sit in the wagon bed.
The dog follows behind. In town, the horse is hitched to a
post. Few ride in on horseback.

Most families with land own horses. The animals run
loose the year around. They are not given feed; they are left
free to graze, even in winter, when they must root the weeds
from beneath a blanket of snow. They become thin. All times
of the year the animals may be seen roaming over the yards of
residents at the Agency, or across the hospital grounds, seeking the best places to graze.

Nearly all families have many mongrel dogs. The dogs
also get little to eat. They are as thin as the horses. The older
Indians eat young boiled dog meat on certain festive and
religious occasions. For a stew, dogs are usually boiled whole,
with the hide on.

The philosophy of the Yuwipi religion used to satisfy the
Indian's everyday needs. If bad luck, famine, or ill-health
came to a man or his family, it was the wish of the Great
Spirit, and the doings of evil spirits. If good luck came to the
family or an ill person recovered, it was also the wish of the
Great Spirit. With so many Indians still primitive-minded,
the old religion still serves as a sufficient comfort.

Yuwipi is conducted by the medicine man. The Indian
family may offer up prayers for the prevention of illness, or
ask that some family member who is ill be healed, but the
medicine man is the medium through whom desires and
thoughts are sent to the Great Spirit, and messages from the
Great Spirit to the family are transmitted in return.

Herbs are preserved as medicinals, even today. Roots of
herbs are dug in the fall and stored for winter use.

The Indian has an unbalanced diet, greatly lacking in
necessary vitamins and minerals, by modern standards. Beans,
rice, bread, and coffee are his usual fare. In spite of this, the
Indian body has excellent recuperative powers. Against
tuberculosis, however, the Indian shows little resistance.
This disease is the scourge of the Indian people. Trachoma

has been virtually conquered, but tuberculosis remains a problem. One difficulty in reducing its prevalence is the attitude the Indians have to hospitalization and to disease. They do not understand the germ theory. When they feel well, they cannot believe something may still be wrong with their bodies. They sign themselves out of the sanitorium before the disease is arrested or cured.

A sick Indian will go to the hospital, but as soon as he feels better, whether he is or not, he wants to leave. He does not understand that convalescence is part of the healing process. Likewise when an Indian fractures a bone and immobilization in a plaster cast helps to eliminate the pain, he will take off the cast and throw it away as soon as the pain is gone.

At Pine Ridge, a resident doctor was assigned, sometime prior to 1900. Up the hill north of the town, on the other side of Cheyenne Creek, not far from the path that today is Highway 18, lived a sick Indian. He was a terminal tuberculosis case. He sent a friend to get some medicine from the doctor. The physician, knowing the case, told the friend that the Indian was going to die. All he could do was make him a little more comfortable. When the friend returned with some tablets, he told the diseased man what the doctor had said. Thinking the white doctor had put a curse on him, the Indian decided to take a white man's life in return for his. The next day, a white man who taught at the Holy Rosary Mission, a little farther north, rode by on his way to the Agency. The sick Indian spied him. He shot the teacher, then went up the hill, east of the trail, and killed himself. He is buried in an unmarked grave at the spot where he took his own life.

An Indian who leaves the tuberculosis sanitorium endangers everyone in his community with whom he comes in contact. Since the tribe must conform to the health laws of the state, it is legal to confine those who refuse treatment. There is an agency that handles these cases. It does not take long to persuade an Indian infected with tuberculosis that treatment is better than confinement. This may help the situation, in time. At present, however, tuberculosis is one of the most common causes of death among the Indians.

The Indians practiced preventive medicine in the old days, but their methods were based on superstition. As they walked across the country together, a young Indian boy might notice his father suddenly elevate his shoulders and draw his chin down, as he passed over a gopher mound or hole. If the youngster asked why, his father would say, "The gopher will protect you from lumpy neck (scrofula or tuberculosis of the neck glands) if you hide your neck when you pass his hole."

The Sioux population is increasing rapidly. Men and women who are parents today were children in families where half the number of babies born died at an early age. In their own families as in their parents', the average number of births will be eight to ten, but more of the children will live. The larger number of children will require an expansion in school facilities, welfare services, and other facilities unless the people leave the reservation. The prenatal clinics and child care offered by the United States Public Health Service has not only decreased infant mortality but maternal mortality as well. One woman not yet thirty recently gave birth to her sixth set of twins. She has had two single births also.

Gall bladder and thyroid gland diseases are common. The Sioux are in the thyroid belt, so called because of the low iodine content of the foods produced. Trauma is common, a frequent result of being injured by a horse. Injuries in motor accidents are fewer in number. Occasionally, there are slashings with knives, and shootings.

The frequency of diarrhea presents problems for the Agency health service. The diarrhea season lasts through the late summer and early fall, the rodeo season. Flies are prevalent. Common eating utensils, poorly cleansed and left standing where flies are abundant, are the undoubted sources from which the bacteria spread. Improper methods of sewage and food disposal also increase the hazards, especially at large gatherings.

The Indians idolize the kind of life a cowboy leads. They like their rodeos to last a long time. They protract the events that are an afternoon's entertainment at an ordinary rodeo into a three-day session. They are never in a hurry.

Doing things the slow way carries over in all their planning and work. One man on the reservation has been building a single-room log cabin for three years. Time does not bother the Indian. He thinks he has an abundance of it, more of it than anything else. Most homes do not have clocks or calendars. The Lakotas seem to have no conception of time, and there is no word for it in their language. The word adopted to express time is "the moving iron," and it refers to the pendulum. The expression "by Indian time," to describe the characteristic way in which Indians disregard fixed appointments or dawdle over their work, is in common usage. Meetings always start late and last long. When an Indian is confronted with a task to perform, he never considers how long it will take, or when it may be completed. The Indian enjoys the moment in which he lives.

He never thinks of tomorrow: where he will be; what he must do, where he will live, or how.

The Indian males of today dress like cowboys. They wear large hats. Shirts fit close, and the colors are bright. Snaps are favored over buttons. Trousers are tight-fitting denims. High-heeled, narrow-toed boots are common. In haircuts, the crew cut is the choice among the younger men. Long, braided hair is worn only by some of the old-timers, especially the full bloods. A kerchief tie about the neck is standard. All Indians tattoo their skin with ink, usually on the backs of the hands, and the arms. Initials and small designs are preferred.

Young girls wear their hair straight with bangs, or long with braids. Many women have long, braided hair. Women's

styles change less than men's. The long, calico dress, with the
shawl in summer and the blanket in winter, thrown over
the shoulders, is the usual sight. Beaded moccasins are typical
footwear.

Old-time family relationships have been retained to
some extent. When two brothers marry, the children of each
family are not cousins but brothers and sisters. But when a
brother and a sister marry, the children of each family have
a cousin relationship.

There is strong rivalry and competition between brothers-
in-law. If a brother-in-law does not annoy his sister's husband, he is not considered virile. For example, one man disrobed an intoxicated brother-in-law and covered his body
with thick grease. Not long after the two families were together at a dance. The man who had been greased told his
brother-in-law that his house was on fire. The alarmed family
quickly went home. They found their house intact. The
rivalry often extends to physical violence and injury.

Some men still do not look their mothers-in-law or sisters-
in-law in the face. When sitting in the same room with them,
any question or comment directed to female in-laws is referred to some other person in the room.

Children rule the home. Their position is also a carry-
over of an old cultural pattern, when children and parents
were on an equal footing. Children have a vocal part in plans
concerning the family and themselves. The grandmother is
the disciplinarian. Children often live with their grand-
mothers. There are instances in which, after one member of
a family, mother or father, dies, the grandmother of the
half-orphaned children has produced a "will," which leaves
the children to her. These handwritten "wills" are usually
faked by the grandparent.

Another survival relates to travel. When a man has to
leave the reservation on business, his spouse must go along.
And since federal funds are not available for both, they
solicit money from people on the street, until enough is
obtained to buy a second ticket.

Family customs had their advantages long ago, but today they are often a nuisance. Family relationships were so intertwined that no one was ever really orphaned. Everyone had a family. A child whose mother died became the child of the mother's sister. Quite often a man married his wife's sister after the wife's death. Family life used to be the basis of Sioux life. No one went hungry. As long as there was food in one family all stragglers were fed.

The most esteemed position in the family was held by the male who became a warrior and went off to war. Today, a soldier is honored by the tribe. Many Indian youths look forward to a call from the draft board. If they are classified 4-F, they highly resent it. They never worry much about their appearance until they are summoned before the draft board; then they become concerned. In the old days, the warrior fought naked or wore only a breechcloth, unless he feared he might be killed; then he dressed in his best war clothes.

During World War II, one youth called to report to the draft board had no decent clothes to wear. His plight was deemed so serious that an old man gave up a month's relief check, and proper clothes were bought for the boy. Returned soldiers are dined, feted, and honored by dances and celebrations.

The Sioux claim to be the inaugurators of democratic practices. They voted by ballot and had woman suffrage before the appearance of the palefaces. A tribe was governed by the chief. That position, as leader and ruler of a band, was hereditary and passed from father to son. If no son was born to succeed the chief, or should a chief be killed before he had established a family, an election was held. The election was attended by great ceremony. The ballots were sticks of wood, about a foot long, and each person, including the women, received one. If three men were running for chief, there were three piles upon which the people could deposit their sticks. After the balloting was over, the man on whose pile the greatest number of sticks had been tossed was the new chief. There were subchiefs and a governing body made up of brave men and warriors appointed by the chief. Membership in this body was not hereditary. One large tepee was designed as the "capitol." It was never used for living quarters, only for council meetings.

The Sioux Nation remained hostile to the white man even after the treaty of 1868. By this treaty, the white man promised certain concessions to the Indian in return for land. Peace was promised. The reservation then included the Dakotas, and parts of Nebraska, Wyoming, Montana, and Minnesota. Agencies had been set up even before this time, to distribute rations and keep an eye on the Indian. The Red Cloud Agency was the first one. It was located on the Platte. Years later, it was set up at Fort Robinson, near Crawford, Nebraska. The chief of a tribe remained the leader, and the representative with whom the government transacted business.

Gradually, the white man began to take over more land than had been promised, until the present reservation boundaries were laid down. In 1879, the Black Hills were signed over to the white man by Red Cloud. The Indians still maintained their own form of government within their group, subject by this time, of course, to the approval of the Agent. These Indians were known as the "friendlies" to distinguish them from a small group of "hostiles" that still roamed free of the white man's control.

Most of the Sioux were under control of Agents by 1889, when, on May 2, Congress enacted the legislation for a trusteeship that was to change their form of government. Land had been allotted and deeded in trust to each person. The head of a family had been given a certain number of acres that, on his death, became an estate and was passed on to his survivors. Each family was given cows, horses, a wagon, pick-axes, shovels, sets of harness, and fifty dollars in cash, to set them up in a permanent living place. Before this they had led a nomadic existence.

The trusteeship was intended to be only temporary, to

last only until they were able to govern themselves under the new form, with a president, vice president, and so on. The setup was unsatisfactory, however, because the president of one community would proclaim himself president of the whole reservation, while another community president would make a similar claim. There was no specific time for elections and no definite length of time that an official served. Elections were called at the discretion of the Agent.

The trusteeship was to expire in twenty-five years, but it was renewable at the discretion of Congress, if the Indians had not learned, by that time, how to govern themselves. At the end of the first twenty-five years, it was extended for ten years more. It was extended a second time, and as expiration neared it was still evident that many Indian groups, especially the Sioux, had not progressed far toward being able to conduct their own affairs.

The Howard-Wheeler Act, passed in 1934, permitted tribes to elect their own officers every two years, and reservations to incorporate to carry on commercial enterprises. These procedures are still in force. However, the Agent of the reservation must approve all bills before they can become laws of the reservation. Any group of Indians are to be so governed until they are able to live in normal competition with white man's society, then the Bureau of Indian Affairs may withdraw.

Pine Ridge is the only reservation where the superintendent of the Agency is a member of the executive board. This provision was enacted by the tribal council.

The Bureau of Indian Affairs was originally under the War Department, having been started in 1824. It was transferred to the Department of the Interior on March 3, 1849. The program and the policies of the Bureau have always had the rehabilitation of the Indian as an end, though the results have not been satisfactory in regard to the Sioux.

Chapter II

THE OLD

(SAMPI YAYA)

WHEN AN INDIAN CHILD WAS BORN, he was not always given a name immediately. Sometimes he was several years of age before he acquired a name of his own. Before the federal government started to record Indian names, family names were nonexistent. After the first census of the Indians, in 1886, they were required to have a family name. Thereafter, the father's name was usually taken by the other members of the family and all gave themselves a distinguishing first name.

Before 1886, a family night have been composed as follows:

> *Black Elk, father*
> *Yellow Hair, mother*
> *Sitting Bear, first son*
> *Eagle Louse, first daughter*
> *White Face, second son*
> *Sitting Hawk, second daughter*

After the census ruling, with its new names, it could have been like this:

Jim Black Elk, father
Mary Black Elk, mother
John Black Elk, first son
Nancy Black Elk, first daughter
Edgar Black Elk, second son
Victoria Black Elk, second daughter

Fathers or mothers often named their children after something that had attracted their attention when the child was born: Two Sticks, Brown Bear, Bushy Top Pine, or some other object observed. Brave deeds or unusual skills were also used as names, like Kills Straight, Kills In Water; or an acquired reputation, like Kills Good; or battle wounds, like Little Wound, Bad Wound. Children named years later were often given a name descriptive of an event of peculiar circumstance in their early lives, like Under the Baggage, Trouble in Front, Walks Under the Ground.

Names were sometimes acquired in amusing ways. One day an Agent was interviewing an Indian through an interpreter, who had paused for several minutes after asking the Indian his name.

"Come, come," said the Agent impatiently. "What did he say his name was?"

"He Doesn't Give a Damn," replied the interpreter, obviously still unsure of it, as the translation of names was difficult and often faulty. In this instance, the translation of the interpreter was a fair one. But today the family uses the more subtle name of Respects Nothing.

The name Afraid of His Horses was acquired by a man whose horses frightened his enemies, because the animals were believed to have been gifted by the Great Spirit, and that in battle no arrows could pierce them. The name is sometimes heard as Young Man of Whose Horses They Are Afraid.

Some children were named for something they did in the first few days of life. Many of these names were considered in poor taste and unprintable by the early census takers, so they

renamed them, thus there are full bloods with European
r.ames.

Early in their lives, children were tattooed with the
symbol of their band. This was done in early fall, after the
milkweed became dry. The weed was charred and then
tattooed on the forehead of the child, with thin, sharp-
pointed sticks.

The young child was kept close to his mother. He was
first taught the wonders of nature and the tribal superstitions
concerning them. Before he was four years old, he was taught
to pray to the spirits of animals, and to the stars, the sun,
and the moon. Self-preservation was firmly stressed. As he
grew older, he was allowed to take part in campfire conversa-
tions with his elders. The Sioux were great storytellers.

When the young son developed endurance, he tagged
along with his father. The girls remained close to the tepee
and under the care of the older women.

A boy had to learn many things before he could become
a warrior. Tagging his father over the hills, he might see
the older man step hard on the ground and utter, "See a
wauk ee on neeck stie pee." (The spelling is phonetic.)

"What are you doing, Father?"

The father would explained that whenever he saw a
spider he must step on it and say, "Spider lightning will
strike you dead." By doing this, the Great Spirit would protect him from being struck by lightning.

Lightning was caused by the thunderbird, a large bird
that flew out of the hills with its eyes shut. It caused rain
to fall, and, if it opened its eyes, lightning was produced.

Bravery was a primary virtue. To test a young son's
bravery, his father would take him to a stream, catch a turtle,
crack open the shell, cut out the quivering heart, and give
it to the youngster to eat raw. He must do this unflinchingly.

Further tests of bravery came in a boy's teens. One was
the water-bag test. A camp was pitched about three miles
from water. After dark a father would hand his young son a

water bag, and point in the direction the water was. The son's task was to find the water in the dark, fill the bag, and return with it. The darkness, the snap of broken twigs, the rustle of birds, and the swish of scurrying animals might frighten the boy, but he had to complete the mission before he was ready for the next step, which was to go off with the warriors to battle. At first, however, he did not participate in battle as a warrior; he packed supplies, tended the horses, and took care of the camp.

The Sioux did not record their history as some tribes did. The children were told stories of the past by their elders, which they, in turn, communicated to the next generation, and so on. They kept calendars, however. These were pieces of wood or hide, on which the year was recorded.

Each year was designated by some special event. Instead of referring to a numbered year, like the palefaces, the Indians referred to some memorable happening of a winter, which marked the year for them. The year began at berry-ripening time (August).

A fire was started by striking a piece of flint against something that could produce sparks, which ignited the fuzz of dried clover plants, gathered and stored in bags for this purpose. Children watched this procedure with rapt attention. Fires were kept alive but smoldering by piling buffalo chips on them. The Indians could leave camp for days, and when they returned the fire would still be burning beneath the manure. Fire was also started by rolling a stick rapidly between the palms of the hands, while one end of it rested on an old dry tree stump. The heat produced by the friction of the stick against the stump would eventually reach the flaming point.

The campfire was the center around which family life revolved. The grandmother held the honored position. She spent most of her time with the children. It was the grandmother who disciplined the children, but always tenderly. The Indians believed that the grandmother's spirit could help them, just as she had done when she was alive. So children and adults alike prayed to the spirit of the grandmother, after her death. If they wanted to find something they had lost, or wanted to accomplish some deed, they believed that the grandmother's spirit would guide them. If the thing lost was not found, or the deed not accomplished, it was not the fault of the spirit, but their own.

Young girls were taught how to prepare food and make clothing for the family by their mothers. They were taught to measure the foot size for moccasins by making an outline of the feet on tanned leather with a piece of charcoal. Usually, the thickest part of the buffalo hide was used for footwear, the parts that cover the joints of the animal's legs. Footwear from these parts of a buffalo hide would outwear three pairs of moccasins made from other animal hides. Other portions of the buffalo hide were made into garments, or used for drum heads. Some moccasins were made with rawhide soles and tanned-leather sides.

In winter, clothing was made of fur. In summer, men wore very little, usually only a breechcloth. The women wore buckskin dresses. The young girls were taught to work the tanned hide with white clay, found only in certain hillsides, until the hide was white. When they entered their teens, they were taught how to work designs into the buckskin with porcupine quills. The Sioux did not weave fabrics, but there were always feathers to clean and dye, and bones to shape and string. Bones were matched for size and length and strung on long pieces of tanned hide, to make ceremonial aprons, which hung from the neck. The women wore these heavy aprons while dancing.

Before a girl learned to tan hides, which were stretched out on the ground with the fur side down and pegged along the edges to keep them taut as they dried, she had to learn about the soap plant. This plant looks like the yucca plant. It has long, straight, pointed gray-green leaves. It blooms by sending up a stalk of multiple white flowers from the center of the clustered leaves. The root is long and reaches deep into the ground. When this root is boiled in water, a slimy, soapy mixture results. The old men and women used to wash their hair in this mixture to prevent grayness. But the girls added ashes to it and soaked the hides in the thickened mixture until the hair slipped easily from the hides. The soaking process took about a week. The hides were then rubbed for many hours with bone marrow. This was obtained by boiling the bones and, after the fluid had cooled, skimming the grease from the water. The marrow made the hides soft and pliable. To obtain a chamois finish, hides were pulled back and forth around a stick, pole, or tree trunk.

Thread for stitching was also obtained from animals. Down the back, along both sides of the backbone, runs a fibrous tissue that shreds into long, thin fibers. This is called sinew. It makes tough sewing material, when dry.

Before the white man introduced beads, intricate designs were made with dyed porcupine quills. The quills were colored with berry juice and earth dyes. They were then dried and pulled between the teeth, one by one, until they were flattened. The flattened quills were then worked into the buckskin, for ornament.

The young girls helped their mothers make parafleches, box-shaped and purse-shaped containers made of rawhide. The edges were laced together with leather strips and tied. The outer surfaces were painted with berry juice and earth dyes.

In the fall, the girls went with their mothers to pick fruits and berries. They gathered the harvest in leather bags. Some of the fruits and berries were put in earthen or stone pots and ground to a pulp before being put out to dry. Some were dried whole. Others were packed, as a flavoring and preserver, with meats. Buffalo berries, chokecherries, wild plums, and wild grapes provided sweets for the long, cold winter months. Indian turnips and onions were also hung up to dry, along with the berries. Wild-rose berries made a sweet tea, when boiled. Thickened with a flour, the paste became jam.

The principal food, however, was meat. The men killed the animals, and the women butchered them and preserved the meat by drying it or packing it with fruits. Buffalo meat was the everyday meat, preferred by the people. It was the beefsteak of today. Deer, antelope, elk, and other meat was eaten less often.

To dry the meat, it was first sliced very thin and then hung. A certain quantity was usually packed in pouches with berries. A meatball was made by flaking the meat, drying it, and then adding a small amount of fat to hold the flakes together. These meatballs were carried by the warriors going to battle.

The Sioux warriors were accustomed to subsist on very little food for days at a time. The warrior usually ate only once a day, when fighting. And during actual battle he might eat or drink nothing.

In battle, his horse meant as much to him as his weapons. The horse is not a native of North America. It was first introduced into Mexico by the Spanish. Horses were traded until they made their way north. The Sioux began to use them about 1740. The horse was used for travel, hunting, and in ceremonies.

Both the warriors and the women had societies. The warriors' was the White Horse society. It was a mark of distinction to own and ride a white horse. At a society gathering, warriors who were members rode their horses around a large circular course. They sang songs that were promises to protect one another in battle, and to help a wounded or fallen partner.

Their war song is still sung today. It is now called the "Chief's Song." The words are as follows:

> *My friends,*
> *We will go to war,*
> *We will kill our enemies.*
> *We will take their horses,*
> *And bring them home to our people.*
> *We will scalp our enemies.*

The Sioux scalped their enemies. According to their rules, however, the warrior who killed an enemy was not necessarily the one who obtained the scalp. Whoever reached the fallen enemy first had that privilege. Returning from battle, the warriors would tie the scalps to long poles, which they waved victoriously, as they rode into camp.

Scalping was not original with the Indians. It was adopted from the British, who paid a bounty for Indian scalps, in the early days along the New England coast. The savage believed that there was an inherent power in the scalp of an enemy, that all the excellent qualities of the victim went with the hair the moment it was sliced from his head. If the victim was a renowned warrior, so much the better, and the greater was the warrior's anxiety to procure the scalp, for he would then inherit all the bravery and power of the slain man.

The Sioux once freed a man because he had a homely face. The captive was so unfortunate in the features God had given him that the Indians decided not to kill him, least of all take his scalp. They even gave him a horse to speed his departure.

There were victims of Indian raids who were shot, scalped, and lived to tell of it. In 1867, a group of Indians wrenched a rail from the Union Pacific track to wreck a freight train that was due at that point after dark. The train was derailed, and the engineer and fireman were killed instantly. The other trainmen jumped, and ran into the darkness. All escaped but one, who was shot and fell. The Indians scalped him, and stripped him of all his clothes except his shoes and shirt. Early the next morning, the man regained consciousness and remembered that another freight train was due. He ran down the tracks and flagged it. He was taken aboard, given medical attention, and lived.

After a battle, the Indians celebrated the victory. They danced and feasted on boiled dog meat. The warriors decorated their faces with paint. A wife painted her face to match her husband's, but used more yellow and red. Clusters of horsehair dangled from her dress, signifying the number of scalps her husband had taken. The warrior wore tufts of scalps on his ceremonial dress from the heads of his enemies.

A warrior used blue and red paint, decorating his arms and legs as well as his face. He streaked the paint across his forehead and down his cheeks. The number and type of the streaks were usually determined by the number of scalpings and battles in which he had participated. He marked his arms and legs with symbols of thunder, lightning, and the sun.

Paints were made from clay and berry juices. The pigments were made into cakes, baked, ground to a fine powder, and then mixed with animal fat. The clay was obtained from certain strata of the soil. Today, as one rides about the reservation, huge multicolored mounds may be seen in which yellow and lavender and red are especially prominent.

While all warriors decorated their skin with pigments, some also tattooed it. Tattooing called for a great ceremony. A young man of eighteen to twenty winters went without food for three days before such an occasion. During the tattooing his people sang:

> *Let his body be pictured,*
> *His face, his spirit also;*
> *And, O Great Spirit in heaven,*
> *And ye winds, make him blue.*
> *Let him not be bitten by snakes.*

The tattooing was performed by the medicine man, using charred weeds for pigmentation, which was pricked into the skin with sharp, pointed sticks. Inflammation followed. The area was kept well greased until it healed. Tattooing was supposed to give courage, and afford protection from snakes. Later, it was thought to give protection from the lead bullets of the white man.

When a young man took a fancy to a maiden, she might become aware of it by the frequency of his glances, or by the more obvious gesture of his following her to a stream when she went for a bag of water. Courtship was simple, by today's customs. The brave might visit the girl and wrap her in his blanket, as they talked. As soon as a young man was certain he wanted to "catch a girl," he discussed the matter with his father. If the father agreed, he then discussed it with the father of the girl. When the union was decided upon, the boy left his horses at the tepee of the girl's family. There was no ceremony of union. On the "wedding day," the two families simply came together, but the young man would neither look into the face of his mother-in-law, nor speak to her directly.

It was customary to exchange gifts: mothers exchanged buckskin leggings, dresses, moccasins, and ornaments; fathers passed the peace pipe.

The young couple did not leave camp. They lived with his or her folks until they had their own tepee.

A new father-in-law enjoyed testing his son-in-law's powers. He might give his daughter a bow and two arrows and say, "Tell your man to go out and kill a deer."

Unions were also arranged by parents. A story of one attempt has been passed down the years. A chief who thought it was time his son caught a girl noticed a pretty young maiden in a nearby tepee. He called on the girl to see if she would live with his son, who would one day be a chief. Then he went to his son and talked it over with him.

But the old chief began to like the girl, too, and frequently visited her, and engaged her in long talks, with his blanket around her. One day he noticed the girl wrapped in another man's blanket. He was jealous. Sneaking over to the tepee, he discovered that the young man was his own son. He hurried back to his own tepee and waited for his son to return.

"Son," he said, "that girl is really your sister. You don't want her."

The boy lay around the tepee several days, not talking. Finally his mother got him to tell her what was troubling him. "Father says the girl is my sister," he said.

It had never occurred to him to question his father further. The girl's father could have been the chief's brother, and in Indian relationships the girl might well have been his sister, in that manner. But that did not occur to the mother. It seemed to her that what the chief had tried to say was that the girl was his own, not knowing it was only jealousy that made the chief speak so.

"Well, I'll tell you something, son. Your father is not the chief," the mother said.

The chief, who was outside the tepee, heard this. He paused to hear more.

"Someday when I see your father, I'll show you who he is," the mother went on. "I'll go like this." She made a gesture that would indicate who the boy's real father was.

The chief watched. He was worried. He spent the rest of his life waiting to see his wife make that revealing gesture.

Eventually, a young married couple started their family. The mother-in-law would deliver the baby. If the mother-in-law was not living, the girl's mother was the next in line. If the family of the expectant mother was not sure of the services of those present, there was always a woman in the tribe who could be called in on such matters.

As soon as the infant arrived, a finger was put down his throat. He was washed with water. His body was covered with fat from large white owls. Then his face was streaked with red or blue paint. This gave long life and protection from the evil spirits.

Indian children were spaced about two years apart. The warrior did not sleep with his wife for at least a year after a child was born. When the family was under way, the rearing was started by the parents and grandparents with stories about nature and the tribal superstitions they believed in.

There was little crime within a camp. There was very little theft. Families had little in a material way except horses and clothes. It was popular, even honorable, for the Sioux to steal the horses of another tribe. There was no motive for murder except the theft of a man's wife. If such an event took place, there was no trial. Everyone knew who the murderer was. The criminal was ostracized from the band. Occasionally, an offender would commit suicide, but usually he joined another band.

As age approached, the Indian was forced to give up his bow and arrow and his good horses. He would sit around oftener and for longer periods, picking an occasional hair from his chin, as he half dozed.

When an Indian died, he was buried by his immediate relatives. Sometimes he was buried in the ground, sometimes in trees. There was wailing throughout the camp, as a dead person, wrapped in animal skins, was carried by travois to burial. Prized possessions of the dead man were buried with him. Possessions not suitable for burial were given to relatives.

If tree burial was chosen, the body was fastened to the branches by leather thongs. The head of the family smoked the peace pipe, pointed it in the four directions of the horizon, then to the ground, and finally above. After tree burials, the family would return later and gather up the fallen bones, which they would bury in the ground.

The white man encouraged burial in the ground. Up to 1900, many bodies were buried in old trunks. Later, wooden boxes were used, but today ordinary caskets are the custom, and some bodies are even embalmed. Graves were decorated with pretty rocks.

After the death of his wife, the lonely husband often went to a hilltop early in the morning to sing mournful songs to the departed one. It was a release for pent-up grief.

Chapter III

RELIGION

(Okolakiciya)

The Indian religion is Yuwipi. The Almighty is the Great Spirit. He is the Creator and Giver of all life. The Indians look to the Great Spirit for their strength, their health, and the cure of disease and illness. They pray to the Great Spirit. They worship and celebrate him. Their whole life and being is dedicated to him. Without the help of the Great Spirit, or if they should fall from his favor, they are weak, small, and inadequate. Life after death is a part of Yuwipi. Heaven is the happy hunting grounds. It is envisioned in its earthly sense as a life of peace.

The Indians paint and tattoo the swastika on their bodies, but it is a clockwise swastika. It means good luck. Hitler's swastika was a counterclockwise symbol. The eagle in flight circles clockwise. To the Indians, this is orderly, because he believes that, after the Great Spirit created the earth and put them on it, he decreed that the Indian's daily life should be lived clockwise. When the white man came, the Indians brought on their own destruction by stopping the forward, clockwise progression of living.

The Great Spirit is upset when the Indians do not use

the peace pipe in the proper ritualistic manner. The Indians were the first to use tobacco. Before the white man came, Indians did not smoke tobacco for pleasure. Anyone who did, sinned. It was used only for an offering to the Great Spirit. The peace pipe is the symbol of their religion, just as the cross symbolizes Christianity.

Long ago, peace pipes were made from bones. The Indians had tried making them from stones, but they were unsatisfactory because ordinary stones cracked under heat. By a stroke of good fortune, they discovered the great pipe-stone deposit, in Minnesota, where they quarried a red rock that can be easily drilled and used for pipes. It does not break when heated. (The pipestone quarry figures very prominently in the history of the Sioux.) When worshiping, the peace pipe is directed to the east, the west, the north, and the south, because there are spirits in those directions that send the winds. Next it is pointed to the ground, because the Indian swears by the earth, then pointed upward to the Great Spirit.

Long ago, the Indians worshiped in the daytime. Today, the ceremonies take place at night. The present-day service has been perverted. Many Indians think it no longer has any significance. The spirits, they feel, are dissatisfied with present-day Indians because of their association with white men.

The peace pipe was given to the Indians by the Great Spirit. Long ago, it seems, two men were walking along a creek bottom, when they noticed, far off in the distance, a maiden approaching. They went forward to meet her. As they drew nearer, they saw she had long hair that shone like gold. She was beautifully attired. One of the men was a good man, the other was bad. The bad man made a remark about the maiden that was unbecoming. The good Indian said, "Oh, you must not make such remarks about this maiden. I am sure she must be an honorable woman."

The maiden, too, reproached the bad man for what he had said about her. Then she said, "I have something for your people. You must assemble them so I can give them the gift from the Great Spirit."

The two men hurried off to tell the people, and after they had heard, they gathered and waited for her.

When the maiden entered the gathering, she said, "I have a gift from the Great Spirit. It is the pipe with which to make your offerings to the Great Spirit."

She asked the Indians not to abuse their privilege. They were to smoke kinnikinnick (a mixture of dried leaves and bark) and tobacco only when making an offering to the Great Spirit.

The minister is the medicine man, who is also, of course, the doctor. At a meeting hymns are sung. The Indian voice is shrill. Hearing it for the first time, in song, one feels that the sound is being produced under great strain. One waits expectantly for the voice to crack. This does not happen. Nor is the speaking voice hoarse after singing.

Indian songs lack harmony, although rhythm is usually maintained. Melody, in the familiar sense, is also lacking. The only accompaniment to the voice is the drum.

In starting a song, the worshipers first hum through one stanza or verse with high-pitched *ee's, ah's,* and *ah-ee's.* Then a verse is sung using words, the next verse is hummed, the following sung, and so on, alternately.

Between songs, the medicine man offers prayers. They sound as if he were reciting verse. Then he asks the Great Spirit for what help is desired.

> *Great Spirit help me.*
> *I am a Red Man.*
> *Now I am vanishing away.*
> *Great Spirit help me to exist.*

This is not meant to indicate that the Indians are vanishing as a result of the white man, or that their race is disappearing. The word *vanishing* is probably a poor transla-

Dewey Beard

Sun Dancers

Sweat Bath

Medicine Man

tion for the weakness of the inner self. In this song, the Indian humbles himself before the Great Spirit.

Tobacco is an important part of every ceremony. This song is sung when the peace pipe is passed:

Friend, you are to do this.
You are to get in the middle (center) of this earth.
When you do that, pray with this peace pipe.
Your prayers will be given (answered).

If a service is held to heal a particular person, a "rosary" is prepared beforehand by the person to be treated. It is made of little pouches of tobacco, wrapped in cloth and tied on a string, about one inch apart. At the end of the string is some "medicine" tied in buckskin. These "rosaries" are offered to the medicine man before the service. After the service, he takes them to a high hill as an offering to the Great Spirit.

The medicine man prepares the altar in the home of the person to be treated, or the person who is asking for help of whatever sort. Then the medicine man is hooded with a blanket, tied up with rope, and laid on the floor, face down, by his helpers. The lights are put out, and windows are covered.

The services vary in procedure. Some medicine men manage immediately to loosen the sinews that bind their hands and then untie the rope around their bodies. In this case, the lights are relit in about two minutes' time. Other medicine men wait until the service is over. If the lights are relit a few minutes after starting, they are put out again soon afterward, and the rest of the ceremony is performed in darkness. Medicine men who slip their bonds tell the worshipers that the Great Spirit has freed them.

Before any ceremony begins, pictures or statues of a religious nature, jewelry, silverware, or anything else made by white men is taken from the room. It is then ready for the people, who sit around on the floor. Sounds are then heard, as of doors opening and shutting. Sparks spring to life in the gloom. They represent wandering spirits. They tap people on the shoulders or head. The spirits seem to have a hairy or furry touch. Gourds filled with pebbles are rattled. Drafts of air sweep through the room, as if a door had been opened quickly, but no door is open.

A pot of hot rocks is carried in, and water is poured over them to make steam, as it is done in a sweat bath. Sprigs of sage are woven into each person's hair, to prevent evil spirits from invading the body. Sage is also rubbed on the hands and face so that anything of good omen that enters may be grasped.

After the service, the lights are lit and the peace pipe is passed around. Then a pail of water and a communal drinking cup is brought. This is the signal that it is feast time, and dog meat is served.

Inikagapi is the Yuwipi ceremony that "renews the body to life." It is the sweat bath. It is conducted in a special structure, separate from and outside the home, made of long, flexible willows saplings, which are stuck into the ground and bent inward to form an igloo-shaped hut. These supports are covered with blankets and canvas. Long ago, these structures were covered with leaves and branches to hold in the steam. There are many sweat baths on the reservation.

The diameter of a sweat bath, at the ground, is about six feet. In the center is a hole in the ground, about a foot deep. Rocks heated until they are red hot, in a fire outside the hut, are placed in the hole. Water is then poured over them, and steam is produced. Years ago, a special kind of rock was used, which would not break or chip, when cold water was added.

The participants in the ceremony enter the sweat house naked. The medicine man offers tobacco to the Great Spirit in return for continued health or for a cure. Outside the sweat house, the "rosary," a string of small pinches of tobacco tied in cloth, hangs permanently.

The ceremony is much like the usual service. Songs are sung. The medicine man talks to the Great Spirit. The peace pipe is offered up. Medicine men make a substantial living from their services. They receive money, food, and other articles.

Sweat-bath meetings are held in the dead of winter as well as the summer months. The "bathers" work their emotions to fever pitch. At one time, sweat baths were located near a stream, and after the ceremony the Indians would jump into the water, even in sub-zero weather. (The Crows, in Montana, still do this.) After the ceremony the body is dried with a cluster of sage leaves.

The sweat bath is recommended both for prevention and cure. The Great Spirit may be asked to prevent illness from coming to some home, or to heal some old man who is afflicted, or to save the life of an ill child. A person in pain or showing other symptoms of illness may expose his weakened body to the hot steam and then the quick cooling, in the hope of a cure.

The sweat bath today is used for other purposes, to find something that has been lost, for instance. If the requests are not granted, it is the fault of the individual, not the Great Spirit. Apparently, in some way, he has displeased the god.

The medicine man is often called upon to treat disease outside of a Yuwipi meeting. His power for healing is given him by the Great Spirit. In many cases, he is asked to treat symptoms of a disease, as the sick person is ignorant or unaware of their cause. A person with pneumonia may have a cough or a fever. The medicine man is asked to cure the cough or the fever. A person who has suffered a cerebral hemorrhage may become paralyzed. The medicine man is called upon to treat the paralytic condition.

Sometimes the medicine man is summoned to a sick person's home by a special token. Years ago, the token was a cherrywood stick. Today, it is more apt to be a "rosary."

A certain formality is involved in this procedure. The member of the family who is chosen to summon the medicine man carries a cherrywood stick, usually about eight inches long, to one end of which a small pinch of tobacco is tied in a cloth and secured. As he nears the medicine man, he announces his approach. The medicine man then chants a song. After the song is over, the messenger enters the medicine man's house and describes the illness in his family. Thereupon the medicine man goes with the person to the home. He treats the patient in one of several ways: symbolically, with an effigy or likeness; physically, upon the body of the patient; or with medicines and herbs.

An old woman who has had a stroke, with subsequent paralysis of one side of her body and face, is treated symbolically. The medicine man draws a picture on the ground to represent the woman. To cure the droop of her mouth and the sag of the facial muscles, he beats on the ground repeatedly at the place where the face is outlined, chanting as he beats.

To cure a man with a pain in his abdomen, the medicine man applies his lips to the place where the patient feels pain, and sucks at it. Another man, who after lifting a heavy load has developed a pain in his back and is unable to straighten up, is given a willow twig and told to put it in his mouth and bite on it. Then the medicine man throws the patient over on his stomach and pounds vigorously on his back. During all this, he chants a song.

An old man suffering from constipation is given a small piece of sage wrapped in the bark of a tree. The medicine man blesses it before giving it to the man.

Not just anyone becomes a medicine man. Here is the story of how Willie Wound was given his powers.

In 1939, Willie Wound was a patient in the Agency hospital, with hepatitis. The doctors told his family that he was very ill, and they had little hope of saving his life. When his family told this to Willie, he decided to go home to die. As Willie walked down the hill from the hospital, he had a vision. He saw the Great Spirit, who promised to help him. The Great Spirit told Willie to go up on a mountain-top and stay there for four days, through a storm that would rage.

As soon as Willie got home, he told his family about the vision. He was determined to climb the mountain. His family tried to dissuade him; they said he would die there alone. But Willie wouldn't listen.

Willie started out for the mountain with no provisions except some tobacco and a peace pipe. A friend followed him, begging him to come back. But Willie kept going. In the distance, the two could see a storm coming.

"Willie," said the friend. "there is a storm coming."

"That's why you must go home without me. You will get wet, and I won't."

The friend turned back. As Willie climbed higher, the storm came closer. The wind blew and the rain beat down fiercely. When Willie reached the mountaintop, the rain poured down all around him except at the spot where he sat. Willie had nothing to eat, nothing to drink. He sat there for three days. All this time the wind blew, the rain fell, and the lightning flashed, but Willie remained dry.

On the fourth day, Willie saw a giant approaching. He came up to Willie and said, "I am not the Great Spirit, but he will come." That was all the giant said, then he left.

Presently, Willie saw a white form moving toward him from the next mountaintop. As the form approached, Willie saw what looked like the bones of a human being shrouded in a white cloud.

"I am the Great Spirit," said the form.

Willie lighted his peace pipe and tried to put it where the mouth of the Great Spirit should be. He could feel the resistance as the pipe came against something hard.

Then, out of the cloud, these words were spoken to Willie: "You are to become a medicine man. Your people will depend on you. By the power of the lightning and thun-der, you will be able to heal your people, who have faith in you and in me. I bestow this power on you to cast out evil spirits. Go now to your people."

The clouded form vanished. Willie stood up. Before, he had been tired and weak. Now, he suddenly felt strong. He turned and walked home.

Willie Wound is a medicine man now, ministering to his people's illnesses, and interpreting messages and wishes from the Great Spirit for the people.

That is the procedure by which an Indian becomes a medicine man. The Indian must stay on a high hill four days and four nights, with no food or drink. He takes tobacco only as an offering to the Great Spirit. The Great Spirit comes usually in the form of an animal. To Willie, he came as a clouded form.

The medicine man Horn Chips had a similar beginning. There is usually some precipitating factor, unless an Indian becomes a medicine man by inheriting the duties from a father. Horn Chip's family died when he was young. He went to live with his grandmother. The other children made so much fun of him that he decided to commit suicide. On his way to a lonely spot to end his life, he heard a voice that said it was that of the Great Spirit. The voice told Horn Chips not to kill himself, that he was destined to become a great man. Horn Chips was told to go to a high mountain, dig a hole four feet deep, cover it with boughs, and stay there four days with no food or drink. Horn Chips followed directions. When he was in the pit, he had a vision. A snake came to him from the Great Spirit and gave him his instructions.

Every time a medicine man opens a meeting, he tells briefly about his vision and how he got his powers. When Little Bear, who became a medicine man after his father stepped down, went in quest of his vision, a large snake, about three feet in diameter and nearly ten miles in length, came up to him.

Many Indians went on vision quests, years ago. If an individual had a vision, he was respected by the tribe. When an Indian went on a vision quest, he stayed four days and four nights without food or drink, while he waited for a voice, or vision of prediction. In old days, visions were probably induced by fatigue and fasting. Voices, usually from snakes or giant animals, told of things to come or things to be done.

The tepee came into being as a result of a vision quest. An old Indian saw a cottonwood leaf, which is roughly triangular, fold up into the shape of a tepee. From this, the idea of the tepee as a dwelling was developed.

Teen-agers were sent on vision quests. A medicine man might test a young man he was sending forth by giving him a bladder bag full of water to carry. The bladder bag was tied to a stick, so it could be stuck in the ground. To test the young man's power to resist temptation, since no one on a vision quest may drink, he had to return from the hilltop with the bag still full of water.

Another religion peculiar to the Indians is the Native American Church. This is a "new" religion, which first took root in the Pine Ridge Reservation in 1913. It offers a peephole to peace for a confused group. It has taken the place of the ghost dances, or the Messiah craze, which expressed resentment against prevailing conditions. However, the Native American Church, or the peyote cult, as it is sometimes called, incorporates parts of the Christian religion.

The federal government prohibits the transportation of the peyote plant, but it doesn't interfere with peyote meetings because they are part of a religion. The peyote cult has a state charter for its church, but the charter does not mention the use of the plant. There is no stated permission to use peyote. The dried buttons are shipped up from Oklahoma and Texas, where the plant grows. It will not grow in the Dakotas.

Those who use the plant are reluctant to talk about the religion, not only because they wish to exclude the white man from the ceremony, but because of the general criticism against peyote and the stories that are circulated about its use. The Indians do not talk about Yuwipi because it displeases the Great Spirit to have the white man know about a thing that is sacred to them. Besides, they fear that the Great Spirit might take out his displeasure on them, if they divulged information about sacred things.

Peyote is a combination of the old religion and the new. There are aspects of the Native American Church that are acceptable. It embraces the teachings of the Sermon on the Mount. Its inexcusable part is its followers' belief that peyote cures disease.

At cult meetings, the peyote buttons are chewed. The peyote symbolizes Christ's Body, which the cultists take into their own bodies. The average number of buttons taken by one person during a night ranges from ten to twenty. Some Indians take from sixty to more than a hundred in a night. Peyote has a bitter taste. It produces gastric irritation. If vomiting should occur, it is interpreted as a purgation of sin. Those who lack teeth to chew the buttons, drink a tea made by boiling them in water.

The peyote is a member of the cactus family, and its button contains the drug mescaline. It produces a change in consciousness that provides escape from troubled states of mind. While under the influence of the drug, the Indian is lifted across the Great Divide to the happy hunting grounds. It produces an extraordinary sense of well-being and release from care.

As the meeting progresses, the singing and praying voices mount to a crescendo. This results from the increasing feeling of happiness, a feeling that the singer is living in a new world. The meeting lasts through the night, with only firelight to illumine the scene. There is none of the superstition that marks Yuwipi. By the next day, the individual is tired, and usually sleeps all day from fatigue. Unlike alcoholic intoxication, peyote leaves no hangover. In spite of popular notions, it is not habit forming, and the user does not crave peyote between meetings. The interval between meetings may be weeks.

The buttons cost from two dollars to three dollars and fifty cents a hundred. In 1953, a peyote supplier who had been shipping buttons into South Dakota, was arrested for income-tax evasion. The peyote-cult groups over the reservation raised a great deal of money to help the offender pay his court costs and expenses.

One young man told how he used to steal, fight, and get drunk frequently, until he became a member of the peyote cult. Such habits are looked down upon. The groups pray for ill people. And contrary to another popular notion, the meetings do not become sexual orgies. Mescaline is not an aphrodisiac. It sometimes happens, however, that outsiders take advantage of people at a "prayer meeting."

The medical profession, as represented by doctors on the various reservations, is much against the use of peyote and the practice of the religion, because, for one thing, it impedes the carrying out of an effective tuberculosis program. One Indian described tuberculosis as merely a "bad condition" of the blood, which backs up in the body. Eventually, it dams up into the lungs and comes up into the throat and suffocates a person. Peyote, however, purifies the blood, and thus it can effect a "cure."

A teen-aged girl, diagnosed as psychotic, was about to be committed to the state institution for care and therapy, after reluctant family consent. When the Agency sent an employee to get the girl, her mother decided not to let her go.

"She is cured," said the mother.

"Cured?" questioned the employee.

"Yeah, we fed her fourteen peyote beans." (The dried part of the plant, which is eaten, is often referred to as a bean as well as a button.)

Members of the cult sometimes bring buttons to friends in the Agency hospital.

The taking of peyote transfers a person to a dream world of the supernatural. His reactions vary, depending on the amount of peyote taken and his mental faculties. Those who try it experimentally, or who have extremely visual minds,

may see only vivid kaleidoscopic patterns during the height-
ened activity of the drug. These patterns may be geometric or
otherwise. They may take the form of spots, streaks, spirals,
circles, latticework, or shimmerings. They have motion, and
they change in color.

But I have not found Indian users of peyote who have
these experiences only. The Indian takes peyote to escape
reality. He slips into a surrealistic world. He is transferred
from a material existence to the illusion of a spiritual existence. A person under the influence of mescaline does not
hallucinate. He sees what is present about him. The importance of what he sees is nonrepresentational. Texture,
softness, smoothness, hardness, brilliance of color, line, form,
and flow become important. There is an indifference to
quality (good or bad, large or small, old or new, useful or
nonuseful). The Indian who has been liberated from his
surroundings during the worship period finds his "new"
surroundings highly attractive. Every object is all right; it
is just as it should be.

The user loses his self-consciousness, but he does not become uninhibited. Crusaders with misconceptions of the
drug would have the public believe that peyote is a narcotic.
Pictures of crime and auto accidents are headlined "peyote,"
as if it were in a class with alcohol or marijuana. To my
knowledge, no person under the influence of peyote on the
Pine Ridge Reservation has committed a crime or used
violence toward another, although alcoholics have invaded
a peaceful peyote meeting and raised havoc.

Peyote does not produce unrestrained actions. A partaker
is in complete control of his physical self at all times. He eats
and drinks. While under the influence of peyote, he finds his
body irrelevant, however.

Time is of no essence. The person has no will to act physically, to go here, or to do this or that, although he has full
use of the functions of his arms and legs, and can walk a
straight line. He is at peace, and wishes to be undisturbed.
Speech becomes neither thick nor slurred, although it may

become loud with pleasure in the sheer experience of "feeling" with mind and soul.

The leaping flames of the fire are live explosions of brilliance. The peyote drum is enjoyed for its very being, the flow of curves and form, the tautness of the surface, and the rhythmic galloping of the leather lacing.

There are two groups of the Native American Church. One is Cross Fire; the other is Half Moon. Both are well organized. Their activities originally were quite different, but in recent years each group has adopted some part of the ritual of the other. Today, from church to church within each group the variations are mainly in the service. The Half Moon group varies more from church to church. The Cross Fire group has a wider, more extensive administrative organization, which controls the units or churches, and there is less flexibility in its ritual.

In Cross Fire, high priests direct the activities. In the single church unit there are four mainstays. In the order of their importance, they are the Road Chief, the Fire Chief, the Drum Chief, and the Cedar Chief.

The meetings begin at sundown, usually on Saturday night, unless a special meeting is called to celebrate the fourth birthday of a child or for an illness. The chiefs go into the house or tent first, through an entrance that is always open to the east. The congregation follows.

The chiefs take their places; the Road Chief back of the crescent-shaped altar, the Fire Chief near the fire, at front center, the Drum Chief on one side, and the Cedar Chief on the other. The members sit on the ground, which has been covered with mattresses or straw. The men sit in front, the women along the wall.

On the altar, which is made of earth and stands near the west wall, is the fetish peyote. A line is drawn along the ground the full length of the altar. This is the road of life. The Fire Chief now strikes a match and lights the fire. He keeps the fire going throughout the ceremony. The Road

Chief rolls a cigarette and smokes it. He passes the tobacco to the other chiefs and then to the congregation. They all roll cigarettes. The Fire Chief lights each cigarette, his own last. Each member takes four puffs. The Road Chief then offers a prayer, which is followed by prayers from any in the congregation who wish to offer them.

The peyote buttons are then passed around. Those who cannot chew the hard brown pod, drink tea brewed from the buttons.

The Drum Chief beats out the "Opening Song." Songs are sung by the congregation; each solos four times. (The number four is repeated throughout Indian life. Animals have four senses and the use of four limbs. There are four "corners" to the earth. Four is a magical number to the Indians.)

The buttons are passed around repeatedly. At midnight, the Road Chief sings the "Midnight Water Call." The Fire Chief brings in water. It is blessed by the Road Chief, then passed around. The Road Chief goes outside again. He blows a long blast on a whistle, then four short blasts and a final long blast. He prays, then faces east, south, west, and north, acknowledging the four cardinal points of the earth. The Cedar Chief sings a song and performs the same directional facings.

The Cedar Chief's job is it to maintain a plentiful supply of cedar wood for the fire. He arranges cedar faggots in groups of four, and also keeps cedar seeds on hand to sprinkle on the fire.

If anyone should leave the building or tent during the evening, he must be cleansed of the evil spirits of the outside night, when he returns, by the Fire Chief.

After midnight, the Road Chief preaches a sermon, using a text from the Bible.

At five in the morning, the Road Chief sings the "Morning Water Call." This time, the wife of the Road Chief brings the pail of water. Then, while another woman brings in breakfast, the Road Chief sings the "Quitting Song." The meeting is ended. Breakfast may be eaten indoors, but it is occasionally taken outdoors in nice weather.

The congregation then goes home in a state of ecstasy and sleeps for the day.

Half Moon has only one chief to direct each church. The fire is built by a member, a volunteer, who also sprinkles it with cedar seeds and feeds it with branches. The cedar seeds are used as incense.

The meetings are conducted much as the Cross Fire meetings are, except that no sermon is preached. They do not use the Bible; instead, they use the peace pipe.

But members of Cross Fire believe in Christ. They call him Peyjuta, which is the Indian word for medicine. They pray and sing to Peyjuta. They also worship the peyote plant. Since the peyote plant is also medicine to them, it is not clear to what extent this identification goes. They will explain that, when a Christian is sick, he knows that Christ will raise him up and cure him. Their worship of Christ seems to be more a substitution brought on by present-day pressures and criticism.

The symbol of Cross Fire is the cross. The symbols of Half Moon are the eagle, the water bird, and the turtle. These, they say, correspond to God the Father (the eagle), God the Son (the turtle), and the Holy Spirit (the water bird.) The Holy Spirit is often represented on stained-glass windows of Christian churches as a dove.

The symbols are also represented by a tepee. The water bird's tail feathers are the poles that protrude above the top. The flaps at the top are the wings. The opening down the front to the entrance flap forms the neck and head. On the entrance flap is painted a turtle reaching up to the head of the water bird. At the level of the water bird's neck are three stripes (yellow, red, and blue.) These are painted around the tepee. These stripes represent a rainbow, and above them is a blue background with white spots that symbolizes a storm. At the rainbow, the storm stops. Below the rainbow, there is no storm. Below, at one side of the rainbow, is the eagle (thunderbird), with lightning stripes above its head. The eagle is all-powerful. He can create or destroy. On the other side of the rainbow is the shield with which the eagle protects itself.

The Indians believe that the eagle wanted to create a human being, but it could not penetrate the water to get to the mud at the bottom, with which to make man. The water bird, although it can live on water, could not get to the bottom for mud, either. So the turtle went down to the bottom, brought up mud, and gave it to the water bird, who gave it to the eagle. The eagle then made man.

INIKAGAPI

It was about an hour before sunset. There had been a strong wind all day, but now it was quieting. Red Cloud came to the sweat house with Plenty Wolf, the medicine man. They carried bundles of tarp, old quilted blankets, and even a piece of old carpet. Elk Boy tended the fire. He cut some pieces of wood from a tree trunk and threw them on the fire. White Whirlwind sat on a log. Red Cloud started throwing the blankets, the carpet, and the pieces of tarp over the sweat-house frame. Elk Boy stirred the rocks on the fire. They were becoming hot. White Whirlwind got up, said a few words, and went toward the log cabin, which was nearly a hundred feet to the west. Presently, he came back with a pail of water. Plenty Wolf held the peace pipe and the tobacco bag. He laid them on a small pile of rocks. Plenty Wolf then laid out four tin cans full of dirt, with the labels still on them. (They had held tomatoes.) On top of two of these were sage leaves. After he had put out this offering to the Great Spirit, to come to earth, he went to the north side of the sweat house and took off his clothing. The house was covered, except for a tiny space on the east side, where the fire burned brightly. Red Cloud and Elk Boy sat on the south side and disrobed. Meanwhile, White Whirlwind had scooped some hot rocks into a pail, which he carried in and dumped in the hole in the ground within the sweat house.

The nude men crawled into the sweat house and squatted.

White Whirlwind poured water on the rocks. The tarps and blankets had been secured to the sweat house with ropes and held down with lumber. The entrance flap was closed. The clouds of steam that rose from the hot rocks were trapped in the darkness of the sweat house.

White Whirlwind was the helper. He sat outside and tended fire. The medicine man prayed and rattled the gourd. Songs were sung. The medicine man asked continued health for the men in the house. Spirit noises were heard.

Presently, it got a little warm. White Whirlwind opened the flap a moment to let in a little cool air and daylight. The wet, naked bodies shone with moisture.

The sun had set, but it was still quite light. The moon was high in the sky. White Whirlwind closed the flap again. More songs were sung. And again the gourd was rattled, prayers were said, and the sound of the spirits became audible. The ceremony then came to an end.

Plenty Wolf asked White Whirlwind to light the peace pipe which had been left outside for the Great Spirit. White Whirlwind took a pinch of tobacco from the long, leather sack. He tied the leather thongs at the top. The strips of leather at the bottom moved in the breeze. After he put a pinch of tobacco in the bowl, he took a burning stick, applied it to the tobacco, and puffed on the long pipestem until the tobacco ignited. Then he passed the pipe to Plenty Wolf. White Whirlwind closed the flap once more. The peace-pipe song was sung, and the pipe passed around. "Hau," said each in turn, as he took the sacred pipe. Plenty Wolf told the Great Spirit the tobacco was being offered to him.

Plenty Wolf came out, then Red Cloud, then Elk Boy. They dried themselves and dressed. Mrs. Elk Boy then appeared with a small, black-and-white dog, a mongrel that had been obtained for the ceremony. She painted a red stripe across its nose, then a red stripe from the tip of the nose down the back to the end of the tail, before the dog was choked to death. As all animals have spirits, it is necessary that they go to the happy hunting grounds. And if the dog had not been painted (a form of baptism), its spirit, after leaving the body, would have been shoved back to earth by the old lady with the blue spot tattooed on her forehead who guards the Milky Way. There are two directions that the animal spirit can take, at the Milky Way. The old lady points to the one the spirit must take. The short fork leads to earth, and once a spirit starts down this path there is no turning back. The old lady follows it and pushes it back to earth, when the end is reached. But the "baptized" spirit is directed to the long fork, which is a peaceful journey to the happy hunting grounds.

As soon as the dog was dead, Mrs. Elk Boy threw it on the fire, which White Whirlwind meanwhile had built up. As the flames singed the dog's hair, she scraped it off with a stick. She also turned the dog over, so the flames could burn all surfaces. She kept scraping away at the singed hair, until the heat drew the legs, the skin cracked over the joints, and the body began to bloat. Then Mrs. Elk Boy took the dog from the fire and dragged it across the grass to remove the last vestiges of blackened hair.

Meanwhile, Red Cloud had brought a pail of water to the sweat bath, which he now threw on the fire, to extinguish it. The tarps, blankets, and the carpet were removed from the sweat house and rolled up.

Everyone now returned to the house, where Mrs. Elk Boy gutted the dog, leaving the tail, head, legs, and skin on. Then, after washing it, she threw it into a pot of boiling water.

As soon as the feast was ready, Plenty Wolf, the medicine man, grabbed the head from the boiling water and ate that portion.

YUWIPI

Blankets covered the windows and door. All furniture had been moved outside. Mattresses and blankets had been scattered around the room for the people to squat on. Poor

Thunder, the medicine man, walked in. He was six feet two, and thin. Braids of hair dangled from his head, down both sides of his deeply lined face. Wisps of short hair kept falling over his forehead and face, which he pushed back with a quick gesture. His lower lip protruded upward over his upper lip, which gave him a mean appearance, although he was a gentle person. His helpers, Yellow Boy and Flesh, were both medicine men. Yellow Boy carried in a pail of hot rocks that had been heated on a fire, outside. He poured water over them, from another pail, and steam rose in clouds. Then he brought several sticks to which pieces of cloth were attached (to represent flags) and placed them over the steaming rocks, to purify them. There were four large flags and four small ones. The longer sticks were about two and one half feet in length. A piece of yellow cloth tied to one represented the sun and moon; the red cloth tied to another symbolized the Indian; and the two white ones stood for purity. The four smaller sticks were about eight inches long, and the pieces of cloth attached to them were also yellow, red, and white.

The sacred altar was made at the south end of the small room. A large can of earth, flanked by two smaller cans, had been set in position. At the north end of the room stood two more cans of earth. Yellow Boy stuck the two large white flags into the cans of earth at the rear of the room, one in each. He then approached the altar and planted the large yellow flag in the small can of earth to the east, and the red one in the small can to the west. In the large can, in the center, he placed the four small flags. And in this large can he also placed a pole, three and one half feet long.

Yellow Boy then placed a large bundle of sage, rolled up in a tarp, before the altar. The medicine man went outside and returned with a suitcase. He opened it and took out a peace pipe, which he laid on the altar. He also took a small piece of paper, about a foot square, from the suitcase. Then he dumped some soil on the paper and smoothed it out evenly, with an eagle feather. Next, he tied two bunches of feathers to the long pole in the large center can of earth.

Poor Thunder then put a package of Bull Durham tobacco and a package of rolled cigarettes on the altar, the
tobacco offerings to the Great Spirit.

Meanwhile, Yellow Boy had carried the bucket of water
up to the altar. Then he took a "rosary," about fifty feet
in length, and tied one end of it to the flag in the can of
earth at the rear of the room on the east. From there, he
strung the rosary to the flag in the can of dirt on the east
side of the altar, looped it around the stick, brought it across
the altar to the can of dirt on the west, looped it again, then
strung it to the back of the room, where he first wound it
around the stick in the can of earth on the west, and then the
can on the east, thus outlining a rectangle.

The five people to be treated now gave the medicine man
small, individual "rosaries," which he laid on the altar. Flesh
gave each person a sprig of sage to put in his hair. Then he
ignited a larger branch and waved it in the air. Its fragrance
permeated the room. When the room was full of the odor,
he dropped the branch on the floor and stomped out the
smoldering sparks.

From his suitcase, Poor Thunder now took a quilted
blanket and handed it to Yellow Boy, who hung it on a nail,
at the rear of the room. He then took a length of braided
sweet grass, ignited one end, and waved the smoking weed
through the folds of the blanket. After he had purified the
blanket with it, he waved it about the room, arching it over
each person's head.

Back of the altar, Elk Boy began to warm up his drum.
All lamps but one were blown out. Poor Thunder took some
rope and two balls from his suitcase, and closed it. Elk Boy
began to beat the drum for the first song. Poor Thunder put
his hands behind him, as a large woman came forward. The
woman tied his hands together with a small rope and laced
it between his fingers. That done, she threw the blanket
over him. Then she took the long piece of rope, put it around
his neck, and made a hitch in it. She repeated this operation
around his chest, his waist, his thighs, and just below the

knees. The medicine man began to sing through the blanket, which gave his voice a peculiar, muffled quality.

As he sang to Wakan Tanka (the Great Spirit), Yellow Boy and Flesh came up and stood behind him. When the song was finished, the medicine man told how he had become a medicine man. He explained that the powers the Great Spirit had given him came from the lightning and thunder.

The woman tucked in the loops of rope around Poor Thunder, and then spread sprigs of sage on the floor. Poor Thunder turned toward Yellow Boy and Flesh, who laid him face down on the sage-spread floor. The one coal-oil lamp that remained lit was extinguished. The medicine man began a song again, still in a muffled voice.

The ceremony then began and lasted about one hour. Throughout the ceremony, the voice of the medicine man could be heard in various cadences but always muffled. The room was in pitch-darkness, but here and there little sparks flashed into life and then winked out. Before the ceremony began, floor boards creaked as members walked over them; now they gave no sound. Just before the light was put out, Flesh and Yellow Boy had squatted on the floor among the other people, and sometimes, between songs, their voices could be heard. The sparks of the spirits flashed about the room only during the singing. Also during the singing, the rattling gourd seemed to be making swift rounds of the room. The five people being treated had no privacy. They recited their troubles aloud. Whenever the singing began, the sparks seemed to flash and the gourd to rattle near them. Hairy arms rubbed their shoulders.

After the treatments were over, and all evil spirits had been driven from the bodies of the ill, the end of the ceremony drew near. The atmosphere was tense; the singing became louder and more vigorous. Presently, a number of flashes, accompanied by loud booming noises, twinkled over the altar. The tiny lights drifted slowly upward. The evil spirits had left the house. Immediately, the singing became softer, diminishing in volume. It seemed to express peace and rest. A quick breeze blew through the room.

The lamp at the altar was now lighted. The medicine man was discovered sitting up. The blanket was folded. The Great Spirit had untied him. The "rosary" that had been strung around the room was no longer there. On the flat dirt surface were marks and a diagram, a message left by the Great Spirit, which only the medicine man could interpret.

Poor Thunder got his peace pipe, lit it, and handed it to the person nearest him. She puffed, then said, "Mita kuye oyasin." All the others responded, "Hau!" She passed the peace pipe to the next person, who also took several puffs and said, "Mita kuye oyasin." Then Yellow Boy took the pail of water and a dipper from the altar and passed them around the room. In his turn, each person drank, saying, as he finished, "Mita kuye oyasin," to which the others responded, "Hau!" *Mita kuye oyasin* means that all are one or all are related.

The ceremony was over. A feast of dog meat followed.

HALF MOON

(Hanhepi Wi Okise)

It was dusk when the worshipers entered the old frame house. They could hear the croak of frogs in the distance, but little could be seen in the gloom. They passed through the small living room and into the largest of the three rooms of the old house, where they sat down on the floor. There was no furniture. The walls were bare. The windows were covered. At the west end of the room was a low platform of dried mud, about two inches high and two and one half feet square. This was the altar. Across it, from one edge to the other, a crescent-shaped mound of packed earth rose to a four-inch elevation, at which point a small depression, two inches square, had been made. Back of the mound, a large peyote button had been placed. On each side of the altar stood a coal-oil lamp.

Running Bear was the main chief. He sat behind the altar, with his back leaning against the west wall. In front of him was a bone whistle, a feather fan, a gourd, a staff, and a sack of Bull Durham tobacco. To his left sat Brady, in front of whom were a sack of cedar seeds and some leaves. To Running Bear's right sat Rising Sun. He had charge of a drum, a calico sack of peyote buttons, some paper cups, and a large pot of peyote tea.

Most of the worshipers had brought along small, oblong cases containing feather fans and gourds, which they had set down within reach.

An Indian named Catches went outside. He returned shortly with a scoopful of live ashes, which he placed on the altar in the concavity formed by the crescent-shaped mound. Running Bear picked up the peyote button that was lying on the altar and placed it in the depression at the top of the mound. Meanwhile, Brady had put cedar branches and cedar seeds on the live coals, the pleasant aroma of cedar began to fill the room.

Smoke rose. Rising Sun passed the drum through the smoke. Runing Bear passed the staff, the gourd, and the fan through the smoke. Then he held the bag of Bull Durham in the smoke, withdrew it, and rolled a cigarette. He handed the makings to Brady, who also rolled a cigarette. The makings then went the rounds: to Little Boy, to Black Crow, to Tail, to Running Hawk, to Sitting Hawk, to Deon, and so on around the room.

Catches went outside again. This time he brought in a cedar stick, two inches thick and sixteen inches long. One end was aflame. He handed the stick to Rising Sun, who lit his cigarette with it. Then he passed it to Running Bear, who also lit his cigarette, and then sent it on its rounds, as he had done with the tobacco. The last to light her cigarette was Mrs. Running Bear. Catches took the stick, the end still glowing, and placed it on the altar in front of the live coals.

The worshipers puffed on their cigarettes. Then Running Bear stood up, closed his eyes, and prayed to Wakan Tanka.

As soon as he had finished, Catches gathered all the cigarette butts except those of the three Indians behind the altar. He laid the butts on the front of the altar. The Indians behind the altar laid their own half-smoked cigarettes on the rear of the altar, back of the crescent of earth.

Running Bear then took the calico sack of peyote buttons and passed them around the room. Everyone helped himself. Then he passed the pot of peyote tea and the cups. Nearly everyone took tea also. All then sat back to drink the tea and chew on the hard, dried peyote buttons.

The drum was made of cast iron, about eight inches in diameter at the top. The drumhead was made of tanned leather, stretched taut. It stood on three legs, which represented the three-in-one God. It contained about a pint of water. Around the top of the drum were seven short spikes. A rope fastened to one spike was carried under the bottom of the drum and up to a spike on the other side, to which it was fastened and the operation repeated. The completed effect was a seven-point design that symbolized the Sacraments. The tightly drawn rope also kept the drumhead taut.

The peyote drum is beaten rapidly with a regular rhythm; there is no syncopation or variation in tempo except at the very end of a song. The drum is beaten with a small unpadded stick. Before each song, the drummer tilts the drum quickly so that the water inside will moisten the leather. He holds the drum in his left hand, with the fingers held flat against the side and pointed downward, while the thumb presses firmly on the surface, and is moved from the periphery toward the center of the drumhead to alter the pitch. When the thumb exerts pressure near the periphery, the leather becomes less taut and the vibrations fewer. The pitch is low and hollow. As the thumb is moved closer to the center, the vibrations increase and the pitch rises. Wet leather dulls the sound.

Running Bear was the first to sing the four prayer hymns. Rising Sun was drummer. Running Bear held the staff and feather fan in his left hand, and the pebble-filled gourd in his left. His eyes were closed tightly in an expression of pained concentration.

As the drummer beat rapidly and steadily, Running Bear rattled the gourd in perfect time with him. When the first song was finished, the rattle of the gourd changed in tempo as Running Bear changed the direction in which he was shaking it and moved it more slowly. The drummer lowered the pitch and slowed the tempo of the rhythm of the drum. He tilted the drum to wet the leather, then commenced again. Running Bear started the second prayer hymn, then the third, and the fourth.

Running Bear passed the staff, the fan, and the gourd to Brady. Rising Sun continued to drum. After Brady had finished his four prayer hymns he handed the paraphernalia to Little Boy. The drum was then passed to Brady, who accompanied Little Boy. (The women did not sing or drum.)

The sack of peyote buttons and the tea were passed around the room between the hymns.

Little Boy drummed next, while Tail sang. Following this, Tail drummed four prayer hymns, while Running Hawk sang. Running Hawk accompanied Sitting Hawk; Sitting Hawk accompanied Deon; Deon accompanied Elk Boy; and so on around the room.

Between the series of songs the crunch of peyote being eaten was very audible.

Each singer closed his eyes in a strained expression as he sang the hymns, even when the words were simply "Forgive us our sins," repeated over and over again.

The paraphernalia of the ritual is beautifully decorated with beadwork. Running Bear's staff had a patriotic red, white, and blue design at one end. Near the top were several rows of beads, and at the top was a tassel of white horsehair. The bottom end carved and tapered to a spear point. Christ carried a staff as he went about the countryside; thus the significance of the ceremonial staff. Multicolored feathers open from the beaded handles of the ceremonial fans. Tassels of ribbon also hang from them. Some fans have tassels of leather strips. The gourds are highly varnished, and secured to beaded handles.

After the drum and the other ceremonial paraphernalia had gone around the room, Catches went out for another scoop of live coals. Brady took more cedar seeds and branches from the beaded leather sack and sprinkled them on the coals. The drum and the paraphernalia then made a second round. It was now nearly twelve o'clock.

Catches brought in more live coals from the fire outside. Brady sprinkled more cedar on it. All paraphernalia was passed through the smoke of burning cedar again.

Running Bear put his bone whistle to his lips. He blew three long blasts and a series of short blasts. Then all the members who had brought their own fans and gourds joined in the "Midnight Song." Rising Sun did the drumming.

Catches brought in a pail of water and set it before the altar. Running Bear prayed the "Water Call." Catches then handed him the pail of water. Running Bear dipped his cup and drank. He passed the pail to Brady, who also drank. Then Brady passed the pail on.

Running Bear arose, closed his eyes, and offered a prayer to Wakan Tanka.

Catches came forward and picked up a small bottle, which contained ground dried-sage leaves. He rolled a large cigarette in a cornhusk. He lit it with the cedar bow, the end of which had been ignited from the live coals on the altar. After several puffs, he handed it to Brady, who smoked more of it. Brady then arose and prayed fervently and long.

When Brady finished his prayer, Running Bear went outside. Catches came forward and picked up the drum and the ceremonial paraphernalia. He handed the articles to Running Hawk. Running Hawk sang the song of the four directions, while Catches drummed. Meanwhile, outside, Running Bear had been offering four prayers to the winds, north, south, east, and west. When he came in, the midnight ceremonies were completed. It was now one o'clock.

The service was resumed. There was no smoking by the

whole group again. Members who wished to stand and give verbal prayers came forward. They took the Bull Durham, rolled a cigarette, smoked a few puffs, and then launched upon long prayers. From time to time, Catches went outside for more live coals. Brady kept the fire sprinkled with cedar seeds.

The drum and the ceremonial paraphernalia was passed around the room as each worshiper, except the women, took his turn singing, then drumming. The sack of peyote buttons and the pot of peyote tea made several rounds. Many shut their eyes as others sang their four hymns of prayer.

When six o'clock came, all took out their own fans and gourds again, and held as the "Morning Song" was sung. Running Bear again led the singing. Rising Sun drummed. The curtain at the east end of the room was removed to let in sunlight.

Running Bear offered the closing prayer, for which all the worshipers stood. Some went out into the fresh air. Mrs. Sitting Hawk brought in dishes and eating utensils. Sitting Hawk followed her with a big pot of *wasna* (squaw corn, chokecherries and dried meat) for the morning breakfast.

Chapter IV

SPIDER STORIES

(IKTOMI)

THE INDIANS HAVE MANY STORIES that are handed down from generation to generation. Many of them are called *iktomi* stories. *Iktomi* means spider. The stories are similar to the white man's Aesop's fables. The villain of these stories is always the spider.

Years ago when commissions were sent from Washington to confer with the Indians, the Indians would whisper, "The *iktomi* men are coming."

Chief Red Cloud once told me, with a twinkle in his eye, "The *iktomi* was Columbus."

The word is frequently used today. Any person who expects a favor without giving something in return is an *iktomi*.

Here are some *iktomi* or spider stories as they were told years and years ago. They were repeated by the Indians as they sat in groups around the campfire or in front of the tepee. They furnished common entertainment at the social gatherings of the Indians, in the old days.

This first story is called "Big Eater."

Long ago, there was a giant. He was huge. He was called Big Eater.

Big Eater had a big head, big ears, and a huge mouth into which he stuffed people, with his big, hairy hands. The Indians always ran when they saw him.

In one band, there was an Indian who bragged that he was the bravest of them all, and that he had supernatural powers.

Another Indian in the band said that if the braggart was so brave he should go and kill Big Eater.

The braggart was taken aback. Nevertheless, he said he would go after the giant, so he started off for the hills. He wasn't certain he'd find Big Eater, but, sure enough, there the giant was.

"Hello," said the man, as he approached Big Eater.

Big Eater didn't answer, but looked at the man with very mean eyes. Every time he blew out his breath, the man could feel it. He walked closer; so close, in fact, that when Big Eater inhaled he drew the man right up to his huge nose, so the man could see inside it.

Then Big Eater gave a big exhalation, and blew the man across a stream of water.

"Look! You don't scare me, Big Eater," said the man, and he walked around on the top of the water.

Big Eater had never seen a human do this before. He watched the man carefully, and became intrigued, then astonished. The man again went up close to Big Eater. "How old are you?" he asked.

"I came when the sky and earth came. I am your creator," Big Eater told him.

"Really? Isn't there anything you're afraid of on this earth, then?"

The man had won Big Eater's confidence, when he had surprised him by walking on the surface of the water.

"Yes," answered Big Eater. "I'm afraid of loud noises. If I ever get too close to loud noise it will kill me."

"What about thunder and lightning?"

"I know when they are coming and I get into my cave."

"Do you get hungry?" asked the man.

"Yes," answered Big Eater. "I'm hungry now, and I'm going to eat you."

"I'll tell you something. Let's go down the big canyon there, first."

Big Eater started off with the man. They walked till they came to a deep canyon, with overhanging edges.

"I'll go scouting and see if I can find a lot of people. I'm hungry, also, and I like to eat people. But I won't scare them as you would. We'll get a lot of them."

The man walked out over the hills. He came back presently and said, "Big Eater, I found many, many people coming this way. You wait here at this end of the canyon. I'll bring them up here and tell them there are lots of buffalo up this canyon. You be here at the head end. I'll herd them and start them up the canyon. When they get to you, you start eating them, and I'll start eating them from behind, until we meet."

The man went out to get his own people. He called them together and told them he had killed Big Eater. But before they could see the dead giant, he said, it would be necessary to drive the bad spirits away. He told them to form two groups, one to proceed along the cliff on one side of the canyon, the other to do likewise on the opposite side. Both groups must then run along the sides of the canyon, where Big Eater lay, and scream as loud as they could and beat all the drums that could be found in the camp.

The groups started. As they neared the place where Big Eater was crouched down waiting for them to come up the canyon, not expecting them to appear on the cliffs overhead, the man gave the signal for them to make lots of noise. The din was earsplitting and Big Eater fell over dead.

This next *iktomi* story is called "The Spider and the Fat Ducks."

There was once a spider going across the country with all his belongings in a sack slung over his back. Presently, he came to a small lake, where he saw some ducks. One of the ducks asked him, "My friend, where are you going?"

"I'm going to a far-off country."

Another duck asked him, "What do you have in the sack?"

"I'm carrying songs to people in the far-off country who like to sing."

"Teach us the songs," several ducks said.

"I will, I will. Come out of the water first. That is fine. Now stand in a line, right in front of me. Do as I tell you, now."

"We will," said one of the ducks.

"Now," said the spider, "shut your eyes tight. If anyone starts the song and opens his eyes before finishing it he will get red eyes, and they will stay with him all the rest of his life. First, I will tell you the words. Then you can sing them. Keep your eyes shut, now. Here are the words:

> *Shut, shut, shut,*
> *Tight, tight, tight,*
> *Dance, dance, dance,*
> *Round, round, round,*
> *Shut, shut, shut.*

The ducks started to sing the song. Then they began to dance, still with their eyes shut. The spider, meanwhile, was taking each duck in turn and wringing its neck. Just before he got to the last duck, the duck realized that he was the only one singing, so he opened his eyes to see what it was all about. When he saw that all his fellow playmates had been killed, he flew off.

The lonely duck felt foolish, but he said, "At least, I'm wiser today than yesterday. Hereafter I shall keep away from such people as the spider."

The spider then sacked the ducks he had killed and started on his way. Presently, he decided it was lunchtime, and he wanted to eat. He laid down the sack of ducks and began to pick up sticks to build a fire with. He then dressed the ducks and put them under the ashes. While they were cooking, he decided to take a walk. Soon he came to a big tree that was singing. He said, "Mr. Tree, teach me the song you are singing." And he laughed.

"I will," said the tree. The tree made a noise by swishing and swaying its branches. "Now," said the tree, "put your hand into this large crack in my trunk."

The spider did. At that moment, a wind that had been blowing stopped, and the tree trunk stopped moving, too. The spider's hand was caught in the crack. He began to plead with the tree to free him.

While the spider stood there, helpless, Mr. Fox came by and saw him. He also smelled the ducks. He hadn't eaten for four days, and he was very hungry.

The spider saw him sniffing around the fire. "Take care, Mr. Fox. You will get your paw burned," he called.

Mr. Fox did take care. He waited until the spider had fallen asleep. Then, when the ducks were cool, he grabbed one, and ran off to the bushes to have a feast. After he was finished, Mr. Fox sneaked back, and as the spider was still asleep, he took the other ducks to carry away for his family. But he returned the bones from the ducks, which he buried in the ashes.

The wind started to blow again. The spider woke up when he heard the noise. Then the old tree trunk started to sway, and the spider got loose. He ran up to the fire, not knowing that Mr. Fox had taken all his ducks and sneaked only the bones back. He dug into the ashes. "Lo, nothing but bones! They have all been cooked to pieces! Oh, ho! I know. Mr. Fox did this. No one cheats me. I'll get with him."

He started on his way and began to sing. The song went like this: "Whoever plays a trick on me, he shall die in the path I take; this shall be your fate, Mr. Fox, cunning creature who pretends to be a friend of mine." And sure enough, he came upon Mr. Fox lying dead in his path.

This following story is called "The Spider and his Cape." There was once a very well-dressed spider who covered his body with a large bear-robe cape. One day, while walking through the hills, the spider became very hungry. Soon he came to a large rock. He covered the rock with his bear-robe cape and prayed to the spirit of the rock, asking it to provide him with food in return for the cape.

Then the spider started on over the hill without his cape. Sure enough, the rock was giving him food. There in his path was a deer, freshly dead.

"Aha!" said the spider, "I'll go back and get my cape. Then I'll come back and eat the deer. That way, I'll have both my cape and the food."

The spider hurried back to the rock. He took his cape, threw it over himself, and hurried back over the hill. But when he got to where the deer had been it was gone.

The spider was very hungry. What should he do? He decided to go back and give his cape to the rock again. This time, he would leave it with the rock. The spider was rather sorry for what he had done. Slowly, he went back to the rock.

Once again, the spider covered the rock with his bear-robe cape. "Spirit of the rock, I am sorry. I'll leave my cape for sure this time. Please give me something to eat. I only came back for my cape because I thought I might get cold. Besides, I didn't think you would need it." The spider had not exactly told the truth.

Once again, the spider started over the hill without his cape. But this time, when he reached the place where the deer had once lain, it was not there. The spider decided to go on a little farther. But still he found nothing to eat. He finally decided to go back and get his cape, since this time the rock did not give him any food. There would be another rock to give his cape to, somewhere.

When the spider reached the rock, his cape was gone. This made him so mad that he kicked the rock and broke his foot. It made a cripple of the spider for the rest of his life.

Chapter V

HUNTING

(Wamkasqan Ole)

The Sioux diet was game meat, wild berries, and fruits. The men hunted and killed the animals. The women dressed the meat, cooked or preserved it, and picked and preserved the berries and fruits.

The Indians killed animals only for food. The mainstay of the tribe was the buffalo. Its meat was their staff of life. Very little of this animal was wasted. The hide made tepees and clothing. The bones made tools and implements. The horns were made into spoons. The bladder was used as a container. Even the buffalo chips were gathered and used for fuel. The head was dried and used as a ceremonial head-dress.

Before the white man came, buffalo were numerous. They roamed in herds, and the Indians, in groups, attacked them on horseback. Horses were trained to dart to the left or right of the buffalo in response to a jab from the rider's foot, or a tug on the single strap tied to the horse's jaw. Usually, the horse was brought close to the left side of the animal. An arrow was then shot in a direction that the hunter hoped would carry it through the hide, back of the last rib, and on toward the head to enter the lungs and heart. If the aim was good, the animal would die shortly. But should the arrow only penetrate the thick, soft tissues of the shoulder muscle, where it could do little damage, the wounded buffalo was apt to become greatly enraged, and turn and charge the warrior's horse.

Beyond Rockyford, there is a tongue of land called Holdout Table that extends out into the Badlands. A number of Indians fled to it in the 1890s, to prepare for their last major show of resistance to the white man. The Indians also used to capture eagles in that region. The Sioux hunted eagles for their feathers, which they used on their war bonnets. Their eagle trap was ingenious. First, a hole was dug in the side of the clay cliff. It was covered with sticks and leaves. The carcass of a skinned rabbit was then tied to a short pole, held by an Indian inside the hole, and the bait was thrust up above the hole covering a few inches. When an eagle would swoop down and fasten on the bait, the pole holder would pull it in and grab the eagle. Sometimes an Indian had to crouch in a hole for days before he got an eagle.

The primitive Indians had rules that had to be observed in hunting. Violators were punished by paying as forfeit some personal possession, usually a horse.

There was also a special season for hunting. The chief of the tribe bestowed regulatory powers on an "advisory group" in all matters concerning the hunt. If a member of the tribe was found guilty of hunting out of season, he most likely would have to give up one of his horses, which was then killed or given to someone else by the advisory group.

The hunting seasons were generally in the spring and fall of the year. Indians did not kill young game, just as they did not kill beyond their needs.

The Black Hills especially abounded with buffalo, deer antelope, coyotes, rabbits, prairie dogs, prairie chickens, porcupines, badgers and beaver, and ducks were plentiful along the streams. An Indian boy got his first hunting practice on rabbits and birds. Then he was allowed to hunt deer. To get a deer, a deer path was covered with vines. The deer was then driven to this spot where, temporarily entangled, it became an easy target for the young arrow shooters.

Hunting was the special task of those men of the tribe who were young and strong. They began learning how to hunt in early childhood. The most skillful were sent on hunting expeditions equipped with the best bows and arrows, lent them by the older men.

When the time came for a hunt, the advisory group first sent out a scouting party to report on the prospects. The Indians traveled much of the time, following the game, or exploring new game fields. If a hunter returned with no game after an expedition, he had to suffer the humiliation of being banned from the elite group. He might even have to give up his bow and arrow. However, he could be reinstated to his former position by again proving his proficiency in marksmanship.

Deer hunting was accomplished in several ways. The deer were often scouted by the medicine man. He marked the area by placing a stick in the ground. The hunting party would then encircle the animals, frighten them, and stampede them toward a high, steep bank which they would be forced to leap, killing themselves.

It is also told that some Indians would dress in deerhides, smear themselves with gall from the scent glands of captured deer, and then infiltrate a herd. It was easy to shoot arrows that killed, with this advantage.

Deer meat was not eaten as often as buffalo meat. It was only an occasional indulgence.

The antelope fed on flats and in the open country between darkness and dawn. When daylight came they slipped into the hills and the Badlands. They were hunted with bow and arrow. A hunting party would form two groups; one group would be stationed at a likely entrance to the Badlands, while the other would work the antelope toward the waiting group.

Few Indians ate coyote. They were killed chiefly for their hides. Nor did the Indians eat badger or skunk. Dried skunkhides were used for arrow pouches. The Indians refused to eat badger meat because the badger ate human flesh, and wherever they found a badger hole they considered it a grave. But the Sioux believed that by killing a badger they could predict how long they would live. The badger was laid on its back and slit open. The entrails were removed. The pooled blood was left to coagulate. Then, the jelled blood was used as a mirror. If he who looked into it saw a youthful-looking image reflected, he would die young; if the reflection appeared to be that of an aged person, he would live a long life.

Beaver tails were eaten, and the hides were made into bags to hold loose hair. The Indians believed that if a hair fell on the ground, it would be eaten by a snake, and sickness would then come to the person who lost the hair. Thus they carefully put all loose hairs that came out in combing into a beaver bag. The bag of hair was always burned when it was full.

The hunters were highly skillful with the bow and arrow. The Indians believed the story told by a medicine man that the Great Spirit had shown him how the Indians were to make arrow-shaped pieces of rock for killing game. Thus their skillfulness was a matter of course, since the use of the arrow was directed by the Great Spirit. The stick portion was made of matured wood; the arrows from flint. Not all arrows had sharp points; some were blunt.

Arrow making, as practiced by the ancient Sioux, is a lost art. There seems to be some difference of opinion about how it was done, but it is generally believed that the arrow flint was chipped by a globular stone, then its edges were flaked with a piece of bone until they became sharp. The Indians believe that arrowheads were originally made by the Great Spirit, and that they had so much power that one would kill a buffalo. The conviction that one arrow was sufficient to kill derived from the belief that the arrow was

a power from the Great Spirit. The Sioux found natural
arrowheads ready for their use when they came to the plains.
(One man told me that once, in Canada, his father heard
in the night a repeated crackle, as arrowheads were made
naturally. He came across a piece of flint that was nearly
arrow-shaped, and marked the place. Returning to Canada
a year later, he went to the spot he had marked and found
that the piece of flint had become a perfectly shaped arrow-
head.)

The piles of arrowheads the Sioux found on the plains
and attributed to the generosity of the Great Spirit were
left behind by cliff dwellers, predecessors of the Sioux, according to anthropologists. Some Indians say that the arrowheads found in a natural state were made by the iktomi, or
spider. Scientists assert that the spider secrets saliva that can
work on flint.

With the coming of the white man, the Indians acquired
knives, guns, and traps. They stopped making arrows, and
thus later generations did not learn the art. Trapping also
was gradually abandoned by the Indians, for guns seemed the
better method for killing game. Human scent on traps was
overcome by rubbing them with cedar branches. The Indians also rubbed cedar branches over their moccasins, before
making the rounds of their traps. Until 1953, an Indian was
not allowed by law to own a gun, although it was seldom enforced. While the statute collected dust on the lawmakers'
shelves, the Indians stacked their own shelves with firearms,
with little interference.

Chapter VI

SIOUX DANCES

(LAKOTA WACIPI)

THE INDIANS DANCED OFTEN, but not for recreation or amusement. Dancing was a part of their religion. Dances were performed to ask favors of the Great Spirit, or to offer thanks for favors granted.

One of the most spectacular dances was the sun dance. It was discontinued in 1881 by the Agent at Pine Ridge Reservation because of its inhuman aspects. It was revived in 1936, but more for ceremony than for real worship.

The sun dance was held in midsummer. It was performed to propitiate the sun. The principal participants in it were young men who wished to gain the sun's favor. A young man who wished to take part in the dance had to make it known to the tribe about one year in advance. He immediately obtained the respect of those in his camp.

When a young man signified his intention to take part in the next sun dance, he lived a good life free of "sin" for his people. His declaration that he would dance was also his announcement that he would live a life of sacrifice. Thereafter, he was looked up to and revered by the other members.

When midsummer came, the tribes gathered in a large

circular enclosure walled by pine limbs and bows. Its entrance looked toward the east. The young men were sent to cut down a very choice tree for a center pole. They chose one that was tall and straight, and its removal from the forest was surrounded by ceremony. The final blow of the ax that toppled it to the ground was delivered by a maiden who was chaste.

To the top of the pole, a number of leather thongs were tied, as many as there were men who would take part in the torture dance, and the effigy of an Indian, complete in all physical details, significant of the phallic nature of the ceremony.

The first part of the dance was performed by maidens claiming virginity. They danced around the pole. Any girl challenged by a warrior had to prove her chastity. If she could not meet the challenge, she was beaten by the other maidens.

The young children were taken behind the enclosure and their ears were slit.

The medicine men then called together, in a tepee, the men who were participating. They were then led out to the center pole. The medicine man explained the purpose of the dance. These great men were offering repentance to the Great Spirit for misdeeds, or asking for provisions to satisfy the needs of the people. Although it was legal to kill an enemy and the proper thing to do, a warrior would nevertheless dance the sun dance for forgiveness of his deed. The dance was to please the sun, and to offer thanksgiving for cures of the seriously ill. As Christ sacrificed his blood, the Indians who danced the sun dance sacrificed their blood and flesh.

A stick of ashwood that had been whittled down to a very sharp point at one end was laid on the hot coals of the nearby fire. The medicine man, with his left thumb and indexfinger, then grasped a pinch of skin and subcutaneous tissue on the chest of one of the young men. Holding in his right hand the pointed stick that had been heating on the fire, he plunged it through the gathered skin as though he were pushing a needle through cloth. A leather thong was then passed through the two perforations, which were about an inch apart, and tied. The other end of the thong had already been tied to the top of the center pole. As each man who was taking part in the dance stepped forward, in turn, the medicine man repeated his office. The men then walked backward until the thongs were drawn taut. Then they gave a jerk backward. Next, they walked a few steps forward, then the same number of steps backward, which tightened the thongs again, and again they would jerk them taut. This rhythmic "dancing," forward and backward was kept up continually. All this while, they kept their eyes upon the sun. With their faces turned skyward, they prayed to the sun.

The men also blew on flutes made of eagle bones. (The flute is the only other musical instrument besides the drum that the Indians use.) These tubular bone instruments produced only a whistle, not several tones, so no tune could be played on them.

The young warriors prayed for the material things desired by the tribe. The dancing continued until the thongs tore loose from the skin, releasing them from the leather strips. Some freed themselves in a few hours, others kept up the rhythmic jerking for a full day. Some tied heavy buffalo skulls to their backs, to give added weight to the pull. Maidens sometimes jumped into the ring and pulled with their braves. If a man fainted and had to be cut loose, he suffered great loss of pride, general indignities, and much embarrassment. Throughout the dance, the young men took neither food nor drink.

The sun dance today is no longer a religious dance, with special significance. It is more like an ordinary get-together. The Indians love to congregate and dance and feast. They still wear gaudy headdresses and war bonnets. Their dancing is a mixture of the old and the new. A few can dance the hoop dance. The Omaha dance is old. The owl dance and the rabbit dance are modern. Men and women pair off and go around in a circle, taking small, rhythmic, mincing steps. Some put in an added step of syncopation by going forward two steps and back one.

The words to the modern dances convey very modern feelings. The verses to the rabbit dance, for instance, are as follows:

> *You are not single,*
> *But you made me like you.*
> *I'm taking your word,*
> *I'll do what you want me to.*
> *You are married,*
> *And have lots of children.*
> *You made me like you,*
> *So I can break up your family.*

The powwow step is used for nearly all kinds of dancing and singing, regardless of the tempo, which usually is fairly constant. Songs are composed for soldiers. One that was composed years ago as a tribute to those who fought in the Custer battle has a very slow tempo.

The steps for the chicken dance are the usual ones, but the body goes through various rapid, vibratory contortions that are patterned after prairie chickens at mating time, when these fowl prance, with their heads cocked at an angle and their wings fibrillating. Some Sioux men can shake their shoulders with a skill that would shame a burlesque queen.

The footwork involves a springing action at the knee, first on one foot, then on the other. The male dancers put one foot on the ground, raise the other, and spring the body up and down from the knee. Usually, only one springing motion of the body is made. Then the balance is shifted, the foot positions are interchanged, and the springing motion of the body is repeated. This is kept up with the feet changing position alternately.

The women keep both feet on the ground at all times and spring the body up and down repeatedly, bending both knees at once. They cover very little ground by just sliding the feet along.

Sleigh bells and sheep bells are a part of most men's costumes. They are strung around the ankle at the top of their beaded moccasins. The women do not wear bells, but the properly dressed woman wears high, beaded leggings that reach to the knee.

In the old days all dancing had a purpose. The maidens' buffalo dance entreated the Great Spirit to make the buffalo plentiful. Virginity was respected among unmarried women. Only those who were chaste, danced. Those who danced and were not chaste displeased the spirits, and the buffalo consequently would be scarce.

Dances were performed before battle to ask for victory, after battle to thank the Great Spirit for their feasts. Scalps taken were tied to long sticks and carried in the dances.

Dances were performed before a hunt and other undertakings to assure their success. Today's dances are called grass dances. Any excuse will serve to hold a dance—a holiday, the return of a soldier, or any other reason that can be thought up.

In the summer of 1953, a family of full bloods who believed in Yuwipi, danced the horse dance, with all the significance of the old ceremonies. It was danced in a secluded spot, well hidden by trees. Many Indians were present. (Three white people saw the dance.)

The Indians believe that when a girl has a dream that signifies bad luck, the spirits are displeased, and only by riding a dancing horse can the Great Spirit be placated and shield the young maiden from bodily harm.

The girl who rode the dancing horse was eighteen years old. She had visions in her dream of being struck by lightning. Her father consulted the medicine man, who advised the girl to ride the dancing horse.

The people congregated. The medicine man appeared. The tom-tom sounded. The medicine man went through a ritual of praying to the Great Spirit. He then led the girl to the center of the secluded spot. She was hooded, a cloth sack having been fitted over her head. A horse was then led to the center of the ceremonial grounds. In keeping with the old ritual, the hooded girl was lifted on the horse, and the animal was made to "dance" by jerking on the reins and kicking it. This done, the Great Spirit was supposedly pleased, and the maiden was protected thereafter against misfortune.

Chapter VII

RED CLOUD

(Mahpiya Luta)

The last half of the nineteenth century brought new and rapidly changing conditions to the Plains Indians. They found it difficult to cope with the problems that arose. The white man poured over their lands; the buffalo began to disappear; their freedom was restricted on all sides.

From this changing order emerged two leaders of the Oglala Sioux who became chiefs. Traditionally, a chieftainship was handed down through the generations of one family until, for one reason or another, the family was disrupted, when a new chief family was elected.

Due to the peculiar circumstances of the time, two powerful men emerged from the chaotic life of the Plains Indians just before they were finally subdued. Their paths separated eventually. One of these leaders, Red Cloud, bowed, at last, to the demands of the white man and became the leader of the "friendlies." The other, Crazy Horse, became the leader of those who resisted. They were called the "hostiles."

In the year 1822, Red Cloud was born near the forks of the Platte River. He was a member of a powerful family.

His father was a man of influence, who had been appointed by Chief Afraid of Horses to sit in council with his people, often called the Smoke people.

Shortly after his first son was born, the father killed an enemy in battle. It was late afternoon, and as he looked up he saw a large, flame-red cloud in the sunset. It was then he thought of his son, and named him Red Cloud.*

Red Cloud grew up to be a good warrior and a good hunter. However, he did not attract much attention from his people until the War of the Outbreak, from 1862 to 1865, when he led the warriors of his people to the head of the Heart River, in North Dakota. There he fought with his kinfolk, the Santee Sioux, in the Battle of Kildeer Mountain, in 1864.

The next summer (1865), Red Cloud was invited to Pierre, South Dakota, to meet with commissioners to make a treaty of peace. A messenger was dispatched to tell Red Cloud that he would be asked permission to let the white men build roads across the western mountains. Red Cloud refused to discuss any such proposal, and he refused to let any of the Oglalas represent the group in the discussions.

Before the council was to convene in Pierre, Red Cloud learned that a caravan led by Colonel Sawyer was on its way to Montana by way of the Platte, south of the Black Hills. A shrewd man, Red Cloud thought a show of force without bloodshed might discourage the enterprising white men. Leading nearly 3,000 braves, Red Cloud caught up with the Sawyer caravan as they were constructing a crossing at the Powder River. He surrounded the men and held them prisoners for fifteen days. Then a young white, Nathaniel Hedges, strayed too far from camp and was killed.

Immediately, Red Cloud noticed signs of unrest in his

_____

* In *McGillycuddy—Agent* (Stanford, Calif.: Standard University Press, 1941, p. 8) it is stated that Red Cloud acquired this name after a battle in which the spilled blood of his enemies covered the ground like a red cloud. The descendants of Red Cloud do not agree with this statement, however.

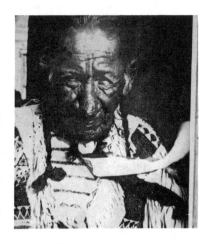

Chief Red Cloud   *The Peyote Altar*

The Battle of Wounded Knee

men. He feared they would kill the entire group of white men. He knew that if this happened he would have a great deal of trouble from the white troops that were bound to be sent in.

Red Cloud turned the whites loose. But he and his group trailed after them. The white men were overtaken again at Tongue River, and again surrounded and held captive, but they were released for the winter. This was considered a remarkable demonstration of self-control on the part of the Sioux.

The Indians began to realize that they were playing a losing game, that their civilization was being slowly destroyed. They decided to listen to a proposition that offered them rations, annuities, and supervision by agents, in lieu of less settled forms of existence. Big Ribs and Big Mouth had set out from Fort Laramie on several different occasions to try to induce Red Cloud, Swift Bear, Afraid of His Horses, and Spotted Tail to sit in council over the existing and increasing difficulties. Crazy Horse always turned a deaf ear to these proposals and enticements. He would have nothing to do with the white man.

A peace commission met at Fort Laramie on June 30, 1866, under a shade built for the meeting. Red Cloud attended and addressed the commission. He refused to consider the building of roads through their hunting grounds, declaring that it would frighten the game away. Then General Carrington arrived with a thousand soldiers. Red Cloud demanded an explanation of their presence.

"To build forts and open the road to Montana," replied Colonel Maynadier.

Red Cloud leaped from the platform and brandished his rifle before the frightened and astonished commissioners.

"In this and the Great Spirit I trust for the right," he cried, and left the council.

Red Cloud protested further to General Carrington, but the general nevertheless proceeded through Oglala territory. Red Cloud then started his campaign of harassment. Carrington built Fort Phil Kearney at the headwaters of the Powder. But it was accomplished under great difficulty, for Red Cloud constantly gave him and his men trouble. The Indians drove off the game, so the white men could get no fresh meat. They stole their horses. On December 21, 1866, Colonel Fetterman went out with eighty-one men to drive Red Cloud away. Red Cloud's and Crazy Horse's groups ambushed the expedition and killed every one of the men.

Red Cloud's men had been attacking Carrington's forces with flaming arrows, which when shot into the wooden boxes around the fort would ignite them, burning them up. Carrington outsmarted the Indians by bringing in wagons with iron sides, or "iron boxes," as they were called by the Indians. In July, 1867, Red Cloud and his men were doubly astonished; first by the iron boxes that would not burn, and second, by the repeating rifles that Carrington's men used against the Sioux for the first time.

Red Cloud lost a great number of warriors. Additional help that arrived for Carrington forced Red Cloud to withdraw. But he kept up the war against the white man.

Red Cloud did not receive his position as chief by inheritance, as was customary. At the time the Plains Indians were being molested by the white man, the chief of the group was Young Man of Whose Horses They Are Afraid (shortened, usually, to Chief Afraid of Horses).

Afraid of Horses was capable and smart, but he was an old man, no longer able to lead his warriors in battle. His son was too young to take over the duties of chief, nor did he promise to be the shrewd leader his people needed at this crucial moment in their history. One of the most able warriors of the Bad Faces (a band of the Oglalas) was Red Cloud, young, smart, and a good fighter. He was called upon so often to lead the Oglalas in battle that the band began to recognize him as leader and follow him. More and more, he was looked to for decisions, and presently he was acting as chief in nearly all functions. By council, he was designated a treaty chief of the Bad Faces early in 1868.

A new peace commission was sent out to Fort Laramie, but Red Cloud refused to join in discussions until the soldiers were withdrawn and the road building was discontinued. The commissioners continued their invitations. Finally, in the late summer of 1868, the government withdrew the soldiers and abandoned construction.

In November of 1868, Red Cloud signed the peace treaty at Fort Laramie. Under this treaty, the Dakotas west of the Missouri River to the Big Horn Mountains, and part of Nebraska, was established as the land of Sioux Nation. The treaty also specified that there would be no more war.

The Oglala Sioux chieftains present at the making of the treaty were Young Man Afraid, Little Wound, Red Cloud, and Spotted Tail. They all signed. For the Cheyennes, Dull Knife and Turkey Legs signed. These chieftains did not wage war with the federal government again, but the bands of "hostiles" continued their harassments. Their leader was Crazy Horse.

On May 10, 1871, under the provisions of the treaty, the Red Cloud Agency was established thirty miles below Fort Laramie. It was a sod hut, thirty by sixty feet. In the autumn of 1873, as a result of the increase of western emigration and the consequent scarcity of game, the Agency was moved eighty miles northeast to White River, at Fort Robinson. The government maintained a sawmill near there. The new Agency was a stockade, two hundred by four hundred feet, with a ten-foot-high wall. A warehouse, thirty by one hundred feet, with a thirty-by-sixty-foot wing, was also erected. There were also three offices, quarters for employees, and several other small buildings.

Red Cloud ceased making war against the white people, but he gave the agents trouble by blocking their plans, arguing and finding fault with everything they sought to do, until the day he died.

In 1877, the year Crazy Horse was killed at Fort Robinson, Red Cloud was asked to move his band to Big Bend, on the Missouri River. After a while, he objected to the new location because the Indians were getting too much liquor from the white men, who came up on the river boats. He was allowed to pick a new spot, and he chose Pine Ridge, where his people still live today. The government built him a good home there, where he lived until his death, on December 13, 1909.

Red Cloud sold the Black Hills to the white man, in 1876. The Indians have held this against him ever since. Many have even maintained that the white man took the Black Hills from Red Cloud, and for years a claim for reimbursement was pending against the government, but on April 5, 1954, the Indian Claims Commission dismissed the Black Hills claim.

Red Cloud gave McGillycuddy, the first Agent at the Pine Ridge Reservation, no co-operation. He declared that the white man had taken the land and game that belonged to the Indian, that the Indians would never work and produce for themselves, and it was up to the white man to take care of them, despite the Treaty of 1868, which stated that services to the Indians would be continued only until they were capable of handling these services themselves, an objective toward which the Indians were expected to strive.

The Indian has progressed little from that time, however. The small log cabins that replaced the tepees look just as they did when they were first built.

Much of Red Cloud's stubbornness and his lack of cooperation with the Pine Ridge Agent was engendered by the squaw men (white men who married Indian women), Janis, Clifford, and Randall. Today, the reservation is well populated by descendants of these three whites. Spotted Tail, from the Rosebud Reservation, told Red Cloud that he was getting a good deal from the Agent and that he should not show so much resistance, but it apparently did not outweigh the council of the white triumvirate.

Red Cloud had only one wife. Polygamy was not uncommon, years ago, but Red Cloud's wife ran other women off, whenever they threatened her position as sole spouse. The chief had eight scalps to his credit. The grandson once remarked, "The white men are no good to scalp; too many bald heads."

Red Cloud was eventually converted to Catholicism. One of his last wishes was to be buried in a black robe, like those the priests and lay brothers wore. It was granted. He had two buckskin outfits, including war bonnets, beautifully decorated with porcupine quillwork. When he died, one of them was sent to Washington. The other is in a museum at the Oglala Community High School, in Pine Ridge.

The second chief, his son Jack Red Cloud, died in the influenza epidemic of 1918. James Red Cloud, his grandson, is chief today. He is nearly eighty. He has never been converted to the Christian religion; he is Yuwipi; but many of Red Cloud's descendants are Catholics.

Chapter VIII

CRAZY HORSE

(TASUNKE WITKO)

THE HERO OF THE SIOUX is Crazy Horse, their greatest warrior. They boast of their relationship to him. They speak proudly, as they say, "Crazy Horse never signed a treaty with the white men." Crazy Horse resisted the Long Knives all his life. When he died, the resistance of the "hostiles" died away, too.

Crazy Horse was born on the eastern slope of the Black Hills, sometime between 1842 and 1844. His father was also Crazy Horse, an Oglala. His mother was a Brule, a sister of Chief Spotted Tail. She died when the child was quite young. His father's second wife was also a sister of Spotted Tail. (It was ordinary for a man to marry his wife's sister, if the wife died.)

The young boy was named His Horse Looking. His father, a medicine man, told the boy tales of the "walking days," of the Chippewa wars, when dog travois were used because horses were few. The boy did not look like other Sioux children. His skin was fair. His features were more like a white boy's than an Indian's. He preferred to watch the elders play the hand game, rather than join in boys' games.

96

The children of the camp made toy dolls and toy travois to haul them on, as they played "packing up and moving." They slid downhill on sleds made of buffalo ribs, and threw rings on the "elkhorns" (a stick with projections). They attached eagle feathers to pieces of decorated buffalo ribs to make darts. But His Horse Looking took no part in these amusements. But he learned to ride early, and often rode into the hills, to sit and think. And he ran with the other youngsters, who followed the women, when they went to eat the raw buffalo liver, as the animals were butchered, after a hunt.

The Sioux bands often fought the Crows and the Snakes, in small encounters, to drive them and other tribes from the Sioux's buffalo hunting grounds. The youngster heard the talk of the white men at Fort Laramie, and the trouble they were giving the Indians.

The bands moved about the Platte continually. It seemed to the young boy that the movements of the bands were always a result of the white man's wishes. In fact, all their troubles were the white man's fault. He began to follow the warriors to battles at a much earlier age than the other youngsters.

His Horse Looking went on a vision quest when he was in his early teens. He stayed away four days and nights without food or drink, but no vision came to him. He started back to camp. When he neared the tree where his horse was tied, he felt faint and dizzy. He sat under the tree to rest for a moment. Then he saw a horse with a rider go swiftly over the hills. The rider had long, flowing hair, not braided, and he wore a feather in it. Behind his left ear was a pebble. The rider was leading warriors into battle. Arrows fell all around him. One killed his horse. He leaped on the horse of a fallen warrior and left the scene of the battle. He had killed many enemies but he had not taken any scalps.

His Horse Looking participated more and more in battles. He became a crack shot. He killed enemies. In the midst of a battle, he would dismount and carry fallen comrades from the field, so they would not be left to the insults of the enemy.

He watched the Battle of Blue Water (September 3, 1855). He was present when Sumner attacked the Cheyennes, on the Solomon River (July 29, 1857). He fought the Snakes on June 20, 1861. He went to the battle of Julesburg (January 7, 1865).

The camp began talking about this young man. Then his father paid him a great honor. He gave him his own name, Crazy Horse.

The young Crazy Horse sat around with the chiefs and warriors. He helped himself to great quantities of *wasna* (a berry-and-meat delicacy), as he listened to their words, but he rarely spoke himself.

Crazy Horse was chosen to lead a group of decoys at the Battle of Platte Bridge (July 25, 1865). For his distinguished conduct in the battle he was allowed to "wear a shirt." Most of the chiefs were old, and their sons were too young or too inexperienced to handle the mounting problems created by the intrusions of the white man. It was necessary to choose men who were leaders. In 1865, Crazy Horse was to be a "shirt wearer" of the Hunkpatilas (a band of Oglalas).

Crazy Horse was an unusual Indian. He never brought back scalps, though he killed enemies. He wore his hair long and unbraided. Around his neck he wore a leather thong threaded through the end of a buffalo horn. In the buffalo horn he carried a small pebble.

Crazy Horse led a raiding party against the Powder River Expedition, at Fort Phil Kearny. The whites were taking the Bozeman Trail, along the North Platte to Fort Laramie, east of the Big Horn Mountains, and on up into Montana.

In December of 1866, he led decoys on the Piney, at Fort Phil Kearny, when Fetterman was massacred. He participated in the Wagon-Box fight of August, 1867, in which Red Cloud gained his reputation as a great leader.

Crazy Horse seemed to be in no hurry to "catch a girl." However, he did visit the tepee of a young maiden and stood in line with others to wrap her in his blanket, but she married someone else. Later, Crazy Horse ran off with this maiden, though she was still married. The incident brought about a split in the band. The girl's husband shot Crazy Horse through the maxilla with one of the white man's guns. Crazy Horse let the girl go. When the wound in his jaw had healed, he led the warriors in skirmishes against the whites and other tribes again.

Crazy Horse often went scouting for buffalo, and usually brought back meat for his band, although game was becoming scarce. Finally, he married Black Shawl.

The great man of the Oglalas had been Red Cloud. But after the peace treaty of 1868, which Red Cloud signed, it seemed to many Indians that he was gradually becoming "white." Crazy Horse was immune to the pleas of those who wanted him to live on federal rations. He grew in stature, to many like-minded Indians, because of his refusal.

In 1874 and 1875, Red Cloud sat in council with the whites and finally agreed to the sale of the Black Hills. Crazy Horse was furious. The white man was trying to whittle their land down to nothing. The Indians must be brought together to resist this destruction.

Crazy Horse was made a chief. With the "hostiles," he roamed the northern country. General Crook and his men were making a trip up the Rosebud, when, on June 17, 1876, Crazy Horse and his men attacked them, forcing Crook to retreat. Generals Terry, Crook, and Custer were to have come together to battle the "hostiles." Custer, however, went ahead to hold them and keep watch on their movements. He felt he could subdue them when he found the group on the Little Big Horn, on June 25.

Crazy Horse and Gall decided to attack. Crazy Horse rubbed soil into his hands, threw some over his horse, and led his men into battle against the soldiers. His voice could be heard above all the others, as he sang his battle song.

This is a beautiful day to die
Brave hearts come die with me.
Weak hearts to the rear.

However, Crazy Horse survived the battle, but not one white man escaped alive.

The warriors fought together. They did not go singly into the foray, seeking personal glory, as they sometimes did. Later, when Army officers questioned Crazy Horse, they asked him if a white man had directed his forces.

Red Cloud and Spotted Tail sold the Black Hills in 1876. That winter was very cold. The "hostiles" were without food, and conditions were becoming worse in every way. More white men were flooding the Black Hills and the adjacent areas. Crazy Horse was wanted by the military now as an out-law. Sitting Bull and Gall had fled to Canada.

Relatives from the "friendlies" at the Red Cloud Agency kept coming to the hostile warrior chief with reports of the good things offered the Indians at the Agencies. Finally, in the summer of 1877, Crazy Horse led his band of Oglalas into the Agency at Crawford, Nebraska. All horses and all guns were taken from the "hostiles." The agent and the military were anxious to talk with the great leader, Crazy Horse. A buffalo hunt was promised. Horses, guns, and am-munition would be given them in the fall, so they could go out for forty days. But Red Cloud, Afraid of Horses, and other "friendlies" were becoming jealous of Crazy Horse. Rumors spread through the two groups. The interpreters (some of whom had once lived with the Crazy Horse group) purposely misinterpreted Crazy Horses's words to the Agent and military, and their words to the chief.

Crazy Horse wanted peace. In his heart, he could never become a "friendly." But the conditions on the prairie could no longer sustain him and his men. He was ready to resign himself to a "captured" existence.

When Red Cloud heard a rumor that Crazy Horse was to be made chief of all the Oglalas, he refused to attend feasts with the "hostiles." Other rumors led the Agent and the military at Fort Robinson to believe that Crazy Horse would fight until all white men were dead.

Crazy Horse went to the Spotted Tail Agency. There he

was persuaded to go back to the Red Cloud Agency, with a friend. As he neared the end of the journey, he became aware that he was surrounded by soldiers. When he arrived at Crawford, he was led to the jail at Fort Robinson. Thinking he was being taken to the Agent's office, he felt that he was a prisoner at last. As he saw the bars of the guardhouse, he turned quickly and drew a knife that had been concealed in his clothing. An Indian policeman stepped up behind him and stabbed him in the back, perforating a kidney. He died about midnight, September 5, 1877.

Chapter IX

THE BATTLE OF
WOUNDED KNEE

(Cankpe Opi Okicize)

The last major armed conflict between the white man and the Indian was the Battle of Wounded Knee, which took place on the Pine Ridge Reservation, December 29, 1890. Various factors brought about increasing tension between the two groups, until it broke into armed battle.

The Indians, in a last desperate chance to rid themselves of the white man, adopted the messiah craze, a religion that they thought held promise of deliverance. Some writers, who have taken the Indian side, lay the blame to broken treaties. That was only one factor. Underlying all more immediate causes were the growing resentment toward the white man's civilization, and his enforced confinement upon them, who had been used to roam at will.

The Indians found promise of escape in the messiah craze, which was also called the ghost-dance religion. They readily espoused this movement because they found in it a release for their pent-up emotions. After joining, many became "hostiles" and fled from the jurisdiction of the Reservation Agent.

This religion that seemed to answer their needs was

102

started by a full-blood Paiute Indian named Wovoka, who lived near Pyramid Lake, Nevada. Wovoka told a story that struck a responsive chord. It expressed feelings and desires that had been struggling for utterance with in them. On January 1, 1889, Wovoka was taken to heaven and instructed to tell the Indians they would be left free to possess their lands. The palefaces would be destroyed. By the spring of 1891, there would be no white man left on the plains, but once again there would be great herds of buffalo.

No better story could have been chosen to confirm the superstitions and unrealistic hopes of the Indian people. In their eagerness to believe, and their confusion, they disregarded the fact that the story embraced part of the white man's religion. An Indian messiah or a savior, a representative of God or the Great Spirit, would deliver them.

The only words the worshipers sang were "Father told us so." They repeated these words over and over, for hours and days, as they danced in a circle about a campfire, often keeping up the singing, without rest, until they saw visions or collapsed.

The moral predicament of the Indian was in trying to retain the old while accepting the new. The inevitable emotional conflict had become a common ailment among the Plains Indians. Different bands of Sioux sent representatives to Wovoka for instructions. The revolt that ensued at first took the form of escape to strongholds in the Badlands. In attempting to dissuade the Indians from running away, the Agencies brought in troops. This disturbed the Indians of the Pine Ridge Reservation greatly, as no troops had been quartered there since it was established.

The Agent and the troops made every effort to quiet the Indians. But the warriors gathered and climbed the hill across Wolf Creek, back of the Agency, from which strategic location they shot down at the Agency and the Indian police. (Today, the Agency hospital is situated on the hill.) The final blow, which put down the demonstrations of this particular religion, at least, was the Battle of Wounded Knee. Wounded Knee is a community on the Reservation.

From that one battle, the Indians today date their downfall. The old preach to their children the indignities the Indians suffered. It is told to youngsters, along with many other stories, to disparage the whites. Instead of improving the present with an eye toward the future, they prefer to evade reality and live on memories, nursing their hate.

On December 6, 1890, after conferences at Pine Ridge with Father Juts, a priest at the Catholic Mission, and General Brooke, of the Army, the leading chiefs of both the "friendlies" and the "hostiles" split the groups even further. Two Strike took his party to the Agency. Short Bull and Kicking Bear retreated to the Badlands.

On December 15, at daybreak, the Indian police on the Standing Rock Reservation went to capture Sitting Bull. He had been intensely active in spreading the message that the Indians would soon be united as a race for a new life of aboriginal happiness. This most influential shaman was about to flee with his followers. Sitting Bull (he was not a chief) was the leader of the Hunkpapa Sioux, but his influence touched all groups. He was one of the greatest stimuli to the uprising.

There were Oglalas in Sitting Bull's group who had fled to Canada with him, where he eluded the federal authorities for a while after his successful campaign against General Custer and his men of the Seventh Cavalry, which ended in their annihilation in the Battle of the Little Big Horn, on June 25, 1876.

The authorities wanted him arrested once again (he had been arrested after his return from Canada, then released) for inciting the Indians to resistance. Had the Indian police gone to Sitting Bull's home just one day later than that December 15, 1890, Sitting Bull would have made his getaway, as he had planned. Instead, in the fracas that ensued when they attempted to arrest him, Sitting Bull was shot and killed. This increased the fears of the agitated Indians and tension mounted. Their greatest leader had now become a martyr, along with Crazy Horse, who had been killed resisting the white man. Many of Sitting Bull's followers escaped to the Cheyenne River and joined the Big Foot band.

The Indians wore "ghost shirts," made of calico and trimmed with a fringe colored with red berry-and-earth dyes. They believed the shirts had the power to resist the white man's bullets. They danced round and round the campfire, singing their only "hymn," "Father told us so." At night, in the flickering flames, they presented a ghostly appearance, with their shirts flapping around them. Emotions were worked up to fever pitch. Some fainted, and water was dashed in their faces to revive them, to dance some more.

Sitting Bull's followers, with Big Foot's, started toward the hideout in the Badlands. On December 25, Kicking Bear, one of the most fiery agitators on the Pine Ridge Reservation, decided to attack the Cheyenne scouts, who were camped on Battle Creek, north of the Badlands. Kicking Bear and his men were driven off.

Orders were given Major Whiteside, of the Seventh Cavalry, to intercept Big Foot's party in their flight toward the Badlands. The flight had already been forced off course by the presence of troops from Fort Burnett, stationed along the west side of this large expanse of tangled clay monuments. The west side had offered the most accessible entrance to the wilderness of tombs and earth spirals that had withstood the winds, snow, and rains of centuries. The group then changed their plans, and turned back to the Pine Ridge Agency, to join Red Cloud and his men.

Meanwhile, refugees were fleeing to the Badlands from the Agency in great numbers. Troops under General Brooke tried to force the Indians back. They were weak from hunger, and no doubt this played a big part in the events of December 27, when most of them broke camp, left the stronghold in the Badlands, and started moving back to the Agency.

Nearing the Porcupine Butte, Chief Big Foot and his people (there were about four hundred in his band) sighted the troops under Major Whiteside's command. Immediately, the Indians raised a white flag of truce. Major Whiteside

demanded unconditional surrender. He then commanded the
Indians to move on to Wounded Knee Creek. Meanwhile, he
had been reinforced by Colonel Forsythe, sent by General
Brooke. The federal group comprised eight troops of cavalry,
one company of scouts, and four pieces of artillery (Hotchkiss
guns). They totaled four hundred and seventy men.

Two Strike and Crow Dog had come to the Agency some
days before with their group. Kicking Bear and Short Bull
had yielded to American Horse and Standing Bear, and also
had decided to come to the Agency.

On the night of December 28, at Wounded Knee, Big
Foot's band made camp. The Army gave them food. In the
center of their camp, the Indians hoisted a white flag. Chief
Big Foot was ill with pneumonia. Colonel Forsythe had
shown him great consideration. He had provided him with
a special tent that was warmed by a camp stove.

The soldiers under Colonel Forsythe's command, who
were new recruits, were stationed on a hill above the Indian
camp, with the four Hotchkiss machine guns trained on it.

The Indians were fearful when they learned that their
camp was under the guns of soldiers of the Seventh Cavalry.
Part of this regiment, under General Custer, had been wiped
out in June, 1876, by this group of Indians.

Shortly after eight o'clock the next morning (December
29, 1890), Colonel Forsythe ordered the Indians to surrender
their arms. The Indians came forward with only two guns.
The soldiers were then ordered to within ten yards of the
warriors. The cavalry was lined up on all sides of the camp.
Another detachment was then ordered to search the tepees.
The troops returned with forty rifles.

There are two versions, three, really, as to what followed.
The third can be dispensed with quickly; it is the explanation of the pure sentimentalists, based on a few nonobjective
manuscripts that put the blame for the first shot squarely on
the troops.

The Indians with whom I have talked (and I have seen
it written) put it this way. One of the Indians was a deaf

mute. When the soldiers came to take his gun, he resisted, not knowing that Big Foot had ordered the Indians to hand over their guns to the troops as they wished. In the scuffle with soldiers, the deaf mute fired his gun. It is said by some that the bullet killed an Army officer. Some Indians, including Dewey Beard, say this Indian was "crazy."

Dewey Beard maintains that if the deaf mute had not been present there would have been no battle. Dewey is a veteran of both the Custer battle and the Wounded Knee battle. He was twenty-seven years old at the time of the fight at Wounded Knee. Bullets went through his left thigh and chest wall. After he fled, he stuffed sage in his wounds to stanch the bleeding.

No Indian remembers the name of the Indian who supposedly fired first, or if they do they will not name him. Maybe it was Black Fox, the name recorded various places in another version (for instance, in the South Dakota Historical Society records).

Here is the other version. Yellow Bird, a medicine man, walked among the warriors blowing an eagle-bone whistle, urging the Indians to resistance. He told them the soldiers were weak. Their "ghost shirts" would resist the bullets of the soldiers. The soldiers, of course, did not understand the Sioux language.

Yellow Bird's words excited the warriors. He stooped down, picked up some earth, and threw it into the air. This was a signal. Black Fox drew a rifle from under his blanket and fired it. Instantly, the soldiers fired volleys into the group.

The air was clouded with the smoke of the soldiers' guns. Colonel Forsythe gave the command to stop shooting, but the fresh recruits fired away at will. They even shot into the group of women and children who had been separated from the warriors.

The morning after the battle, snow began to fall. Thirty-one dead troops were gathered up. Nearly two hundred slain Indians, including women and children, were loaded on wagons and hauled to the hill where the Hotchkiss guns had been mounted. There they were buried in a common grave.

One day while riding through Wounded Knee, my passenger, an Indian, pointed to the bank of the creek and told this story. When the battle was joined, an Indian woman, with her baby strapped to her back, ran to the bank of the creek to hide. A soldier aimed his gun at her and blew the baby's head off. As she crouched under the bank, a soldier was shot nearby. She grabbed his gun and waited. The next person to pass near her was an officer on horseback. She took aim, fired, and hit him squarely in the head, killing him.

A couple years ago, Alice Straight Forehead (née Alice Moves Over), one of the very few survivors of the battle who are yet alive, showed me two scars where a bullet had passed through her left shoulder.

The Indians have no written records of past events. It is difficult today to document certain happenings of years ago. It is known that children were orphaned after this battle. Indian families quickly "adopted" these children. One Army officer who was at the Battle of Wounded Knee found a live baby girl strapped to the back of her dead mother. The officer rescued the little child, gave her the best of care, and took her east to his home, when he left that country.

Chapter X

THE NEW

(LE HANTU)

It is said that cleanliness is next to Godliness, but for us Indians education is next to Godliness. The hope of the Sioux people does not rest in treaties and handouts from the government, but in the education of our boys and girls.

Superintendent Ben Reifel

THE CURRENT TREND in the Bureau of Indian Affairs is withdrawal. To some individuals, the program assumes the proportion of abandonment of the Indians and their problems. Such is not the case, however. Withdrawal is the orderly turning over of services now offered the Indians by the federal government to state, county, and local governments. The Indian will not be left stranded.

The Bureau of Indian Affairs, as it now operates, segregates the Indian. In the light of recent decisions by the Supreme Court on segregation in schools, this fact become even more apparent.

The status of the Indian was changed in 1924. In that year, all Indians were made citizens of the United States. As a group, the Constitution does not provide special services for them.

Segregation of Indians started with the expansion and development of the country west of the Mississippi, when they were confined to reserves in an effort to end their wars and forays. This is seen in the names of the many reserves that begin with the word "Fort."

Reserves were defined by treaties between the United States and an Indian tribe. Tribes were domestic dependent nations. Treaty obligations have been fulfilled. Treaties are not made with Indians now, since a treaty is an agreement with a foreign government (or tribe).

The United States Government has an obligation to these people to do the fair thing, and the proper course, it would appear, should be to allow the Indian, where possible, to receive services others receive in the same way others receive them. According to Superintendent Ben Reifel, of the Pine Ridge Indian Reservation, the Indians wish to be free of the supervision and guidance of the Bureau of Indian Affairs and the federal government.

The policy of the Bureau of Indian Affairs is a flexible one. Some Indians are more developed than others, and withdrawal is taking place in these groups. Some Indians have not progressed sufficiently to come under control of state and local governments. They therefore will not be turned over to these governments at this time.

The Indians are not without opportunity. But opportunity as defined by non-Indians means something else in the Indian's definition. Generally, for the Indian, it means nothing but a lot of hard work. In this light, the government often subsidizes Indian failures. Opportunity and vision go hand in hand for the non-Indian who wants a secure position for the future. But the Indian is satisfied with one pay check, and then will leave a job.

The administration of the Bureau's program in the past has not disregarded the idea of helping the Indian. But in many instances it has not been administered in a way to help the Indian help himself.

The Indians have exercised one privilege of democracy.

They have been unusually vocal in expressing their criticism of the Bureau of Indian Affairs. This has changed recently. The following was written by an Indian for an Indian publication:*

> To some, it will come as no surprise if within a short time we will begin to hear the praises of the Indian Bureau, and why it should not be abolished. And, it will come from those same people who have for years been taking the hide off of the officials who have run the Indian Bureau, and charged it with many errors and mismanagement of Indian Affairs.

The problems of the people are largely economic and social. There is general unemployment since there are no jobs on this (Pine Ridge) Reservation. Generally, Indians will not look for permanent work off the reserve, nor will they stay with jobs for any length of time. For this reason, men with business interests are reluctant to hire such unsteady help. The average able-bodied male works perhaps four weeks out of the year. Many work not at all. Others work longer and then live awhile on unemployment compensation. Income from whatever source is mismanaged. Aside from environmental factors, much of the Indian's poverty stems from immaturity.

Many able-bodied men and their families live from relief money provided by the Agency Welfare Department, or from the checks of a relative or friend who receives state aid to the blind, old-age assistance, or aid to dependent children. Funds such as these are misused. There are other abuses. One judge writes that his court "has no brief for women who use ADC money to get drunk and lie around the house all day while their children are neglected."**

Many Indians receive money from the lease of their land.

---

* *Talking Leaf*, vol. III, no. 8, January, 1954.
** *Daily News Sheet* Pine Ridge Agency, vol. I, no. 68, May 17, 1954.

Those who sell their land, even when they receive thousands of dollars, dissipate the money in a short time. Then they apply for relief. These practices are not isolated occurrences; they are general. Divorces are stopped and engagements made on the strength of impending land sales.

Different Indian tribes vary in their assumption of responsibility. Some groups are economically sound. The group at Pine Ridge is not. Nor could it become economically sound if the members were agrarians, for the Reservation could not provide for fifty per cent of the population now living on the land. Industry brought to the Reservation may solve some of the difficulties. But whatever the help, it must provide a stimulus that will promote the establishing of new standards and concepts very different from those that now prevail.

The white people must show understanding and patience for the Indian and his problems. Especially, a real attempt at understanding the Indian in his state of transition is greatly needed.

The policy of state officials in regard to relocated families has been to send the Indian back to the Reservation and the federal government, whenever he develops into a problem.

The same attitude is held by others. Some say the Indian should not be "assimilated" into society but should be left to his peculiar environment and "tribal rule." Such policies would keep the Indian in an aboriginal state, which is hardly fair to the Indian. There is ample opportunity for a better life for all.

Public officials who shirk responsibility where Indians are concerned prevent the Indians from being treated like others, and close off the road of their progress. The practice of some public officials in communities where Indians have become firmly established uproots the families and sends them back to the Reservation. These officials are only creating future headaches for themselves by not trying to solve the problems of these families in the cities, for more and more Indians will be leaving the reserve.

There is need for public assistance in the United States,

but for individuals, not groups. And this assistance should be administered by the same officials who administer it to non-Indians. Discrimination is retarding the Indian's approach to maturity. Families who live in cities and pay taxes and buy or rent homes as others do are entitled to services in the communities where they reside. That some will encounter economic difficulties is a foregone conclusion.

There are changes taking place on the Pine Ridge Reservation in South Dakota. For the first time in history, the Agent is an Indian. He is Ben Reifel, a Brule Sioux. His theme is "the spirit of our leaders, Crazy Horse and Red Cloud, is dying, but with the help of God we can bring it to life again."

This leader is not only carrying out the rules and regulations of the Bureau of Indian Affairs, he is also making an attempt to instill new and progressive ideas into the Indian people. Agents of the past have not been without progressive ideas, but they seemed unable to get them across to these difficult people. The Pine Ridge Reservation Agency has always been considered the most difficult to administrate. This is not only true of the past; it is a still existent reality. Mr. Reifel says this is so because it is a government by personality, not principle. He has stated that a vocal minority has made it tough for previous agents.

Mr. Reifel is trying to change attitudes by bringing about public censure of common shortcomings. He is a public-relations man. A list is published daily of the names of the people in the jail for intoxication and other offenses. He is urging persons known to be tubercular, who are out of the sanitorium against medical advice, to return for cure. He is hitting at crime. He is urging the people to file complaints against the drunks who enter homes at night, breaking doors, and getting children out of bed and frightening them. Once made, he is urging the people not to withdraw their complaints before they are heard.

In 1953, President Eisenhower signed a bill permitting Indians to purchase and consume liquor, but subject to local censure. The voters of Pine Ridge Reservation voted against liquor sales on the Reservation. The bootleggers were responsible for this, because they make a very profitable business selling liquor to the Indians at more than the off-the-reservation cost. The Indians, however, were quite satisfied with arrangements as they had always been.

Mr. Reifel's policy of enforcing liquor restrictions has been hard on the bootleggers and on the drinkers. So now the Indians are kicking.

As an example of their behavior, one Indian wrote the President about the situation here. The reply he received was that the Indian was not permitted to drink if local authorities and the people did not allow the practice. The next procedure was to call a sidewalk audience, which this person did. He announced that he had written to the Canadian Government to ask if the Sioux could move to Canada. And, he added, only full bloods would be allowed to go.

Enforcing the liquor law has been a great problem. From drinking and drunkenness stems much of the poverty, illness, debauchery, and delinquency.

Mr. Reifel woke one morning to find liquor bottles placed on the fence posts around his yard. He made no effort to remove them. He announced that they would stay there for people to see, as a symbol of the dying Sioux Nation.

Mr. Reifel's theory is that no amount of assistance through health, education, welfare, law and order, or other community services will help change his people under existing discrepancies in the ratio of male to female population. He is making a study of this special aspect of the problem. He feels that since there are so many more women than men on the Reservation existing conditions will not improve until the ratio is equal or reversed.

Relocation of Indian families off the Reservation seems to be an answer to some of the problems. With conditions equal, Mr. Reifel will offer women an opportunity to leave the Reservation in preference to men. In the past, many more men than women have left.

Time is an unimportant factor in the Indian culture. It has little meaning to them. Mr. Reifel is making a great effort to reverse this and develop a sense of the value of time among the Sioux.

Though Mr. Reifel is meeting opposition and his task is hard, he is a man of might. Down under, the Sioux are proud of him. Characteristically, they are jealous of one of their own who makes good. But they recognize him as a great warrior, with the spirit of Crazy Horse and Red Cloud, whose inspired purpose is to erase the depravity that has besmirched Sioux pride and honor, and make the Sioux Nation again the Great Sioux Nation, and not just a name on a gravestone of history.

INDEX